FIGHTING FINANCIAL CRIME IN THE GLOBAL ECONOMIC CRISIS: AN EXPLORATIVE

FIGHTING FINANCIAL CRIME IN THE GLOBAL ECONOMIC CRISIS: AN EXPLORATIVE

Dr. Anne Wade

SOCIETY Publishing

www.societypublishing.com

Fighting Financial Crime in the Global Economic Crisis: An Explorative

Dr. Anne Wade

Society Publishing
224 Shoreacres Road
Burlington, ON L7L 2H2
Canada
www.societypublishing.com
Email: orders@arclereducation.com

ISBN: 978-1-77469-883-9 (Hardcover)

ABOUT THE AUTHOR

Dr. Anne Wad has been a researcher and a professor in the Criminal Justice field for over 30 years. She currently holds a position as a Provost/CAO in a University, and Director of Research at another university. She holds an Ed.D. in Educational Leadership and a Ph.D. in Public Safety Leadership/Criminal Justice. Her research interests are in Criminology, Victimology, and the Human Services. She is married to Wesley Wade. She is an artist, writer, researcher, professor, and university administrator.

TABLE OF CONTENTS

LIST OF FIGURES

LIST OF ABBREVIATIONS

ABS	Asset Backed Securities
ACAMS	Association of Certified Anti-Money Laundering Specialists
AF	Asset Forfeiture
AML	Anti-Money Laundering
ARM	Adjustable-Rate Mortgage
ATOs	Account Takeover Attacks
BBA	British Bankers Association
BSA	Bank Secrecy Act
CAMS	Certified Anti-Money Laundering Specialist
CBDC	Central Bank Digital Currency
CD	Certificates of Deposit
CDO	Collateralized Debt Obligations
CFT	Combating the Financing of Terrorism
CFTC	Commodities and Futures Trading Commission
CPP	Card Protection Policy
CSP	Corporate Social Performance
CSR	Corporate Social Responsibility
DLT	Distributed Ledger Technology
DNFBPs	Designated Non-Financial Businesses and Professions
DOJ	Department of Justice
ECB	European Central Bank
EDD	Enhanced Due Diligence
ESG	Environmental, Social, and Governance
FATCA	Foreign Account Tax Compliance Act
FATF	Financial Action Task Force
FBI	Federal Bureau of Investigation
FCA	Financial Conduct Authority
FCS	Financial Crimes Section

FDIC-OIG	Federal Deposit Insurance Corporation-Office of the Inspector General
FHA	Federal Housing Administration
FinCEN	Financial Crimes Enforcement Network
FIU	Financial Intelligence Unit
FNMA	Federal National Mortgage Association
FOS	Financial Ombudsman Service
FRBNY	Federal Reserve Bank of New York
FSA	Financial Services Authority
FSMA	Financial Services and Market Act
FSP	Forfeiture Support Project
FSRBs	FATF Style Regional Bodies
FX	Foreign Exchange
FY	Fiscal Year
G7	Group of Seven
GDP	Gross Domestic Product
GFC	Global Financial Crisis
GNMA	Government National Mortgage Association
GPML	Global Program against Money Laundering
GSEs	Government Sponsored Entities
HUD-OIG	Housing and Urban Development-Office of the Inspector General
IBA	Intercontinental Exchange's Benchmark Administration
ICE	Intercontinental Exchange
ICOs	Initial Coin Offerings
ICT	Information and Communications Technology
IDV	Identity Verification Software
IMF	International Monetary Fund
IRS	Internal Revenue Service
KYC	Know Your Customer
LIBOR	London Interbank Offered Rate
MBS	Mortgage-Backed Securities
MLU	Money Laundering Unit
NASD	National Association of Securities Dealers
NATO	North Atlantic Treaty Organization
OCC	Office of the Comptroller of the Currency
OMM	Operation Malicious Mortgage
OTC	Over-the-Counter

PEPs	Politically Exposed Persons
PRA	Prudential Regulatory Authority
QF	Quick Flip
RBS	Royal Bank of Scotland
RFPA	Right to Financial Privacy Act
ROI	Return of Investment
RPA	Robotic Process Automation
RTGS	Real-Time Gross Settlement
SAR	Suspicious Activity Report
SEC	Securities and Exchange Commission
SFO	Serious Fraud Office
SOFR	Secured Overnight Financing Rate
SPE	Special Purpose Entity
SPV	Special Purpose Vehicle
SSN	Social Security Number
TALF	Termed Asset-Backed Securities Loan Facility
TARP	Troubled Asset Relief Program
TPB	Terrorism Prevention Branch
UNCAC	United Nations Convention against Corruption
UNODC	United Nations Office on Drugs and Crime
UPI	Unified Payment Interface
USAO	U.S. Attorneys' Offices
USPIS	U.S. Postal Inspection Service
WCCP	White Collar Crime Program

LIST OF GLOSSARY

A

Acquisitive Crime – It is a criminal offense, such as theft, aimed at acquiring property for the offender (Oxford Dictionary of Law Enforcement, 2007).

Aggression – A forceful action or procedure (such as an unprovoked attack) especially when intended to dominate or master.

Anti-Money Laundering (AML) – It refers to laws and regulations intended to stop criminals from disguising illegally obtained funds as legitimate income.

Attacker – A person who uses violence to hurt someone.

B

Bank Secrecy – In respect of a customer, banking secrecy is a privilege, which means that the customer's financial information should be protected legally and should not be invaded by other parties.

Bioethics – It is both a field of study and professional practice, interested in ethical issues related to health, including those emerging from advances in biology, medicine, and technologies.

Bitcoin – It is a form of digital currency that aims to eliminate the need for central authorities such as banks or governments.

Bond – A bond is a fixed-income investment that represents a loan made by an investor to a borrower, usually corporate or governmental.

Border Crossing – A border checkpoint is a location on an international border where travelers or goods are inspected and allowed passage through.

C

Cold War – The Cold War was an ongoing political rivalry between the United States and the Soviet Union and their respective allies that developed after World War II.

Consequentialist – An ethical theory that judges whether or not something is right by what its consequences are.

Corruption – It is a form of dishonesty or a criminal offense which is undertaken by a person or an organization which is entrusted in a position of authority, to acquire illicit benefits or abuse power for one's personal gain.

Counterfeit Currency – Counterfeit money is currency produced without the legal sanction of a state or government, usually in a deliberate attempt to imitate that currency and so as to deceive its recipient.

Crypto – A combining form meaning "hidden," "secret," used in the formation of compound.

D

Digital Currencies – A digital currency is a medium of exchange that is generated, stored, and transferred electronically.

F

Financial Stability – It is a property of a financial system that dissipates financial imbalances that arise endogenously in the financial markets or because of significant adverse and unforeseeable circumstances.

H

Heat List – Chicago's Strategic Subject List/Heat List is a rank-ordered list of people judged most likely to be involved in a homicide or non-fatal shooting.

J

Jurisdiction – Power of a court to adjudicate cases and issue orders.

L

Layering – This in money laundering can be the process of making multiple transactions, in order to hide a criminal's tracks.

Legislative – Belonging to the branch of government that is charged with such powers as making laws, levying, and collecting taxes, and making financial appropriations.

Liability – Liabilities are what you owe other parties.

M

Manipulation – When a person uses controlling and harmful behaviors to avoid responsibility, conceal their true intentions, or cause doubt and confusion.

Money Laundering – Money laundering is the process of illegally concealing the origin of money, obtained from illicit activities such as drug trafficking, corruption, embezzlement, or gambling, by converting it into a legitimate source.

Mortgage – An agreement between you and a lender that gives the lender the right to take your property if you fail to repay the money you've borrowed plus interest.

N

Non-Performing Loan – A non-performing loan is a bank loan that is subject to late repayment or is unlikely to be repaid by the borrower in full.

P

Pfandbrief – The Pfandbrief, a mostly triple-A rated German bank debenture, has become the blueprint of many covered bond models in Europe and beyond.

Ponzi Scheme – It is a form of fraud that lures investors and pays profits to earlier investors with funds from more recent investors.

Portfolio – It is an organized, visual collection of a person's progress, achievements, and efforts that demonstrates his/her accomplishments.

R

Reckless Behavior – A pattern of reckless behavior may involve the following features: Repeatedly going over the limit in almost any activity.

Repackaged Assets – Repackaged products allow investment firms to resell existing assets or securities in a different form.

Revenue – The money generated from normal business operations, calculated as the average sales price times the number of units sold.

V

Virtual Currencies – Virtual currency is a digital representation of value, other than a representation of the U.S. dollar or a foreign currency ("real currency"), that functions as a unit of account, a store of value, and a medium of exchange.

W

White Collar Crime – It is generally non-violent in nature and includes public corruption, health care fraud, mortgage fraud, securities fraud, and money laundering, to name a few.

PREFACE

Everyone can be exposed to financial fraud. If you are selling or buying online, providing financial services, or simply processing tons of payments, you face fraud risks every day. Where there is money, there is been tax evasion, but in the late 20th and early 21st centuries, as globalization fueled the growth of offshore finance, and particularly the use of anonymous shell companies and trusts to conceal illicit activity, there was an explosion in the scale, scope, and level of sophistication of financial shenanigans.

From decades ago, financial crimes have been one of the most important topics on the international stage. Since authorities are constantly attempting to track down and prevent financial crimes, it has always been a cat and mouse game between law enforcement and criminals. Criminals, however, constantly invent new strategies to stay one step ahead.

Financial crime, by definition, is a crime that is specifically committed against property or money where an individual or criminal organization takes something belonging to someone else for their own personal benefit. The most common types of financial crimes are money laundering, bribery, corruption, fraud, tax evasion, forgery, and even terrorist financing.

When considering a financial crime, you need to get rid of the mental image of being robbed at knifepoint while walking down the street or having someone break into your house. Financial crime can be committed by well-respected individuals embedded in our society who perform the crime from the comfort of their own homes or office. When analyzing who performs financial crimes, we can group them into several categories lie employees, business leaders, corrupt heads of state, organized criminals, and customers and suppliers.

With the current climate of economic downturns, global conflicts, and international sanctions, the job of financial crime has never been tougher. For businesses, scams are especially scary because you are not losing money but also customers who may no longer trust you. So, detecting and preventing financial crimes is essential.

The book discusses the current landscapes today for finding financial crimes and what the challenges, both internal and external, are for financial services providers in this space, and how an orchestrated approach solves these challenges.

This book analyzes the effectiveness of the institutional, regulatory, and legal framework for preventing financial crime. The book advances novel and helpful ideas and highlights significant connections between various forms of financial crime and money laundering. It makes clear the types of financial crimes as well as who is capable of committing them. Additionally covered are financial crime's methods, reach, and victims. This book also explains the widespread issues that developing countries face, as well as the negligent automation of law enforcement.

The most important takeaways are the prospect of criminalizing careless risk-taking on the financial markets, the obligation of banks to combat money laundering and corruption, the expansion of the shadow banking system, and bank manipulation of LIBOR. The book exposes the intricate interrelationships between regulatory agencies, law enforcement, and private players to reduce the negative impact of white-collar crime on the stability of the financial sector. It also demonstrates the worldwide character of financial crime.

The book concludes by discussing the value of virtual currencies, the role of Bitcoin as a store of value, potential regulatory concerns, and the connection between distributed coordination and virtual currencies. This book will be very helpful and interesting for experts, practitioners, and students in the fields of financial crime, banking, finance law, and international political economy.

Dr. Anne Wade

Provost/CAO Kenner University;

Dean of Education & Centre for Research and Innovation Charisma University

CHAPTER 1

Introduction to Financial Crime

Contents

This chapter talks about the introduction to financial crime. At the beginning of this chapter, the chapter explains financial crime and types of financial crime. The chapter also addresses the activities and extent of financial crime. The chapter provides highlights on the victims of financial crime, The facilitating factors and priorities of public institutions, relationships among financial crimes, the top six biggest financial crimes, and measures against financial crimes. The end of the chapter explains financial crime risk management and the future of fighting.

1.1. FINANCIAL CRIME

Financial crimes are illegal acts committed by people or criminal groups with the intention of obtaining financial gain. The economy and society suffer huge losses because of financial crimes, which have emerged as a serious problem on a global scale in recent years. A significant share of the global GDP is made up of proceeds from financial crimes.

To combat financial crimes, regulatory agencies continually create new strategies. Additionally, criminals create new strategies as a result of technological advancement. Money laundering, corruption, fraud, and sponsorship of terrorism are currently the most prevalent financial crimes. Crimes that provide financial gain to criminal groups are known as financial crimes.

Typically, in financial crimes, one party receives an economic benefit while the other side loses money. These often include the illegal conversion of ownership of the concerned property and are conducted for the personal gain of the criminal. They can occur in many different forms, and they happen all over the world.

The most common crimes facing the financial sector are money laundering, terrorist financing, fraud, and tax evasion. These offenses are regularly prosecuted by governments around the world as they look for fresh offenders even though they are committed every day.

A universally recognized definition of financial crime does not exist (IMF, 2001; Ryder, 2011). A common definition of financial crime is "crime against property," which refers to the illegal conversion of another person's property for the perpetrator's own use and benefit.

According to the International Monetary Fund (IMF, 2001), financial crime refers to "any non-violent crime that generally results in a financial loss." In the UK, the Financial Services and Markets Act 2000 (FSMA) states that financial crime includes 'any offense involving fraud or dishonesty; misconduct in, or misuse of information relating to, a financial market; or managing the proceeds of crime.'

White collar crime, financial abuse, and financial crime are terms that researchers and government organizations use interchangeably without making any apparent distinctions between them (Figure 1.1).

Figure 1.1. Members of the International Monetary and Financial Committee.

Source: Image by Flickr.

According to IMF (2001), financial crime is a subset of financial abuse and necessitates a financial loss. Financial crime is also fostered by lax regulatory and supervisory frameworks and tax systems.

The phrases "financial crime," "white-collar crime," and "fraud" are all used interchangeably by Pickett & Pickett (2002) to describe the use of deception for illegal gain, typically involving a breach of trust and concealing of the true nature of the activities.

Contrarily, according to Interpol, financial crime is also referred to as "white-collar crime," a term first used by Sutherland (1939) to describe offenses perpetrated by people of high social standing while doing their line of work.

White collar crime corresponds to occupational criminality under this concept. White collar crime also includes financial crime because both are committed by people or groups, regardless of their line of work. Examples of white-collar crime are money laundering, insider dealing, fraud, and market manipulation, which can be captured by financial crime. Governments all throughout the world have grown more concerned about financial crime over the past 30 years. The impact of financial crime varies depending on the setting, which gives rise to a number of concerns. Today, it is generally acknowledged that the prevalence of economically motivated crime poses a serious danger to the growth and stability of many societies' economies.

It is possible to divide financial crime into two essentially different, although closely related, types of conduct.

The first category is comprised of those behaviors that dishonestly produce wealth for the participants in the in-question behavior. A meaningful profit is sought when, for instance, insider information is used improperly, or someone else's property is fraudulently acquired. Alternately, one might use deception to obtain material advantage for another.

Second, there are financial crimes that don't involve deceitfully obtaining a benefit; instead, they work to safeguard an already-obtained benefit or to make it easier to obtain one. An illustration of this behavior is when someone makes an effort to hide the proceeds of another crime from the law by laundering money.

Learn more about joining the international ICA community here if you are thinking about advancing your anti-money laundering (AML) career. By signing up as a member right now, you will have access to a plethora of information, tools, resources, and hands-on support that can help you advance your career.

Being a member of ICA also demonstrates a commitment to the highest standards of practice and conduct and enhances your professional reputation and employability.

1.2. WHO COMMITS FINANCIAL CRIME?

Financial crime may be committed by anyone, including the senior management or employees of the organization, customers, other stakeholders, the general public, or declared criminals. Financial crime may be divided into two essentially different, although closely related, types of crimes.

First, criminals will engage in unlawful activity to obtain money or resources, such as using insider information for their gain or defrauding someone else into giving them their property. Alternately, one could lie to obtain a different material advantage. Second, financial crimes don't entail deceitfully obtaining an advantage; rather, they involve preserving an already-obtained benefit or aiding in its acquisition. An illustration is when someone tries to hide the proceeds of another crime from the law by laundering money.

Companies in all sectors of the economy must be aware of financial crime and those who may be involved in it to safeguard the integrity of the economy and financial system. The requirement for financial system access during pandemic lockdowns has sparked an exponential growth in technology innovation over the last several years, as well as the evolution of digital assets and currencies.

In a globalized world, financial crime has increasingly crossed international borders. With the ability to create, modify, or steal information, digitization is a double-edged sword that presents potential for fraud and money laundering. Along with advancements in technology, money laundering methods have improved throughout time.

Criminals utilize front firms to enter transactions or register accounts because it helps them conceal their identity. In the case of identity theft, fraud risk and money laundering come together, enabling criminals to conceal their unlawful activity by using victims' accounts. These crimes frequently occur together or inextricably link to one another.

There are seven main groups of people who commit different types of financial crimes, which are:

- Criminal groups, including terrorist groups, increasingly perpetrate large-scale frauds to fund their activities and operations.
- Corrupt leaders often make use of their status and authority to plunder their nations' (often impoverished) financial resources.
- Senior executives or business leaders frequently falsify or distort financial data to exaggerate a company's genuine financial situation.
- Employees from the most senior to the most junior steal company funds and other assets.
- Fraud can be committed from outside the corporation by a supplier, contractor, customer, or another individual.
- Increasingly, the external fraudster colludes with an employee to more easily achieve bigger and better results.
- Last but not least, another type of people who have committed a financial crime is the successful individual criminal, serial, or opportunist fraudsters who have their proceeds in hand.

Financial crime can take many different forms, from small-scale thefts or frauds conducted by well-intentioned people to elaborate schemes hatched by global organized crime groups. Because of their widespread connections to violent crime, including terrorism, and their significant social and economic effects, they are major criminal acts that should not be taken lightly.

1.3. TYPES OF FINANCIAL CRIME

1.3.1. Money Laundering

Money laundering is the process of disguising the origin of money earned from illicit activity and transferring it to a legitimate source in order to avoid being prosecuted, found guilty, and having the proceeds of the crime seized. Transforming black money into white money is an unlawful practice.

Money laundering is a serious financial crime. AML measures have gained importance to prevent and curb such practices.

1.3.1.1. Process of Money Laundering

Money laundering is a three-step process, namely – placement, layering, and integration (Figure 1.2):

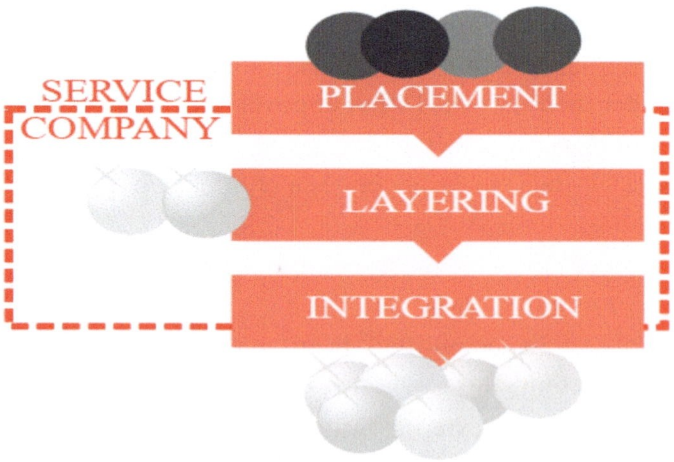

Figure 1.2. Diagrammatic description of a money laundering scheme involving a service company.

Source: Image by Wikimedia Commons.

- **Placement:** At this point, the criminal proceeds are introduced into the financial system by the money launderers. Frequently, money is put into a bank account that is linked to a business middleman or an anonymous entity to do this.
- **Layering:** The money so introduced via placement is moved or dispersed over numerous transactions in other accounts of the same nation and other nations where AML rules are less strict, making it challenging to identify the source of the money.

  Transactions like the purchase of tradable assets like expensive cars, artwork, and real estate can also be included in layering the funds.
- **Integration:** Once again entering the financial system, such strategically placed, and skillfully stacked money erases its prior connection to criminality and is used to subvert the law by appearing to have come from legitimate sources.

The criminal might then use this clean money to fund a legitimate company, claiming payment by creating fictitious invoices, or even launch a bogus charity, where they would be paid extravagantly to sit on the board of directors.

1.3.1.2. How Is Money Laundering Done?

The ways to launder money are always evolving as criminals come up with creative ways to launder their illicit funds. The most commonly used methods of money laundering are:

- **Smurfing:** Criminals engage in smurfing, also known as structuring, when they divide a large sum of money into smaller sums, carry out several transactions, and distribute the money among other accounts to obscure the source.
- **Electronic Money:** Criminals can obtain money in a variety of methods, including by utilizing malware, phishing, account hackers, or other techniques. By making purchases with that money using stored value cards, such illicit funds are frequently laundered.
- **Offshore Accounts:** People with unexplained surplus credit transfer that money into nations with weak or nonexistent AML regulations. As a result of the no disclosure policy in certain tax haven nations, criminals feel secure and break the law.

- **Money Mules:** Equally accountable as the money launderer is the cash smuggler who assists in moving the illicit funds between nations and deposits those funds in nations with laxer tax regulations.
- **Cryptocurrencies:** Money laundering opportunities have expanded as a result of the recently introduced online transacting currency in the shape of cryptos like Bitcoin and several others. A substantial flow of wealth across nations may happen as OTC trade increases. Additionally, certain cryptocurrencies' lax KYC requirements have served as an encouragement for money laundering.
- **Casinos:** Cash is used by money launderers to purchase casino chips, which are then later swapped for checks issued by the casinos, sometimes without any betting or gambling.

1.3.1.3. Prevention of Money Laundering

It is a huge step back for the governments as approximately US $800 billion to US $2 trillion of the estimated amount is laundered globally every year.

In order to combat money laundering globally, the group of seven (G7) countries established the financial action task force (FATF) as an international organization in 1989.

The Bank Secrecy Act (BSA) passed by the United States in 1970 asks financial institutions to report suspicious transactions or cash transactions exceeding $10,000 to the Department of the Treasury.

Through the investigation and prevention of organized crime and drug trafficking, the USA Patriot Act aids in the detection of money laundering and can be useful in the detection of terrorists.

With legislation requiring financial institutions to set up systems to detect and report suspicious activity, governments around the world have increased their efforts to combat money laundering in recent decades. There is a significant financial investment.

According to the United Nations Office on Drugs and Crime (UNODC), global money-laundering transactions account for approximately $800 billion to $2 trillion annually, or some 2% to 5% of global gross domestic product (GDP), although it is difficult to estimate the total amount due to the clandestine nature of money laundering. To combat money laundering on a global scale, the G7 established the FATF as an international organization in

1989. Its scope widened to include preventing the financing of terrorists in the early 2000s.

The United States passed the BSA in 1970, requiring financial institutions to report certain transactions, such as cash transactions above $10,000 or any others that they deem suspicious, on a suspicious activity report (SAR) to the Department of the Treasury.

The financial crimes enforcement network (FinCEN) utilizes the data that the banks submit to the Treasury Department and may divulge it to domestic criminal investigators, international organizations, or foreign financial intelligence units (FIUs).

Although these regulations were useful in identifying criminal conduct, the Money Laundering Control Act was not passed in the US until 1986, making money laundering itself unlawful.

The USA Patriot Act, which passed shortly after the terrorist attacks of September 11, 2001, increased money-laundering operations by permitting the use of investigative instruments intended for the prevention of organized crime and narcotics trafficking in terrorist investigations.

The Association of Certified Anti-Money Laundering Specialists (ACAMS) offers a professional designation known as a Certified Anti-Money Laundering Specialist (CAMS). Individuals who earn CAMS certification may work as brokerage compliance managers, BSA officers, FIU managers, surveillance analysts, and financial crimes investigative analysts.

1.3.2. Terrorist Financing

To assemble their networks of supporters, run their logistical bases, and conduct their activities, terrorists need money. To effectively combat the threat of terrorism, it is essential to stop terrorists from gaining access to financial resources. The technological expertise and operational and legal structures required to identify, look into, and prosecute terrorist financing instances are, nevertheless, lacking in many States.

The International Convention for the Suppression of the Financing of Terrorism (1999) is a particularly important universal legal instrument that the terrorism prevention branch (TPB) of the UNODC works to promote the ratification of as well as the application of these international standards.

This entails reviews of domestic legislation to ensure proper criminalization of offenses related to the financing of terrorism and legislative drafting, developing the capacity of criminal justice and law enforcement officials to investigate, prosecute, and adjudicate terrorist financing through the provision of specialized training on issues related to special investigation techniques, freezing, seizing, and confiscating terrorist assets, and strengthening regional and international cooperation against the financing of terrorism.

A "Mock Criminal Investigation" and a "Mock Trial" on terrorism, terrorist financing, and connections to serious related crimes were developed by the TPB in 2012 as two ground-breaking training tools in Spanish, giving practitioners the chance to simulate trials and criminal investigations based on real-life scenarios.

The "Case Management Tool," also available in Spanish, was later introduced by TPB in 2014 as a useful and hands-on tool for prosecutors and teams of criminal investigators, in accordance with international and national frameworks for each country, for the criminal investigation in contexts of financing of terrorism.

As noted in the UNODC report on the "Use of the Internet for Terrorist Purposes," particular attention is also given to the difficulties that arise in the investigation and prosecution of cases involving the misuse of new technologies for terrorism financing.

To ensure an integrated approach to its technical assistance delivery and the pooling of financial resources and expert knowledge, the TPB works in close partnership with UNODC's Global Program against Money Laundering (GPML), Proceeds of Crime and the Financing of Terrorism (GPML).

1.3.3. Bribery and Corruption

The same justifications and excuses for bribery and corruption, like other white-collar crimes, are heard repeatedly. "Everybody does it," "it's a cost of doing business," "it doesn't really matter," "nobody gets hurt."

This is untrue. Serious moral and political issues are the bribery and corruption of decision-makers in both public and corporate sectors. These crimes do not go unpunished, and they have a significant negative impact on society and the economy. Bribery and corruption damage the social fabric of both rich and developing nations, creating an unfair playing field for legitimate firms.

They can translate into inferior and dangerous products allowed onto the marketplace, substandard building materials used in infrastructure projects that can endanger people's health and welfare, and the diversion of vital money required for education, health, and welfare services.

Although corruption can take many different forms, it always includes the misuse of a public or private office for one's own benefit. A dishonest official may, misuse their power (for instance, when a purchasing manager awards a contract to a supplier who has paid bribes) or neglect to utilize it properly (e.g., where a building inspector ignores the use of sub-standard building that should be reported) (Figure 1.3).

Figure 1.3. Shaking hands with euro banknotes hidden in the hands as a bribe.

Source: Image by Wikimedia Commons.

Others involved in corruption may act for a variety of personal or professional motives. Extremely simple or extraordinarily sophisticated corrupt transactions involving businesses in numerous nations are both possible. At the highest levels of both government and major multinational corporations, corruption is possible. It can also happen at a local level, wherever somebody has the power to influence decision-making.

One of the biggest barriers to long-term economic, political, and social progress in emerging, developed, and developing economies is corruption. In general, corruption causes productivity to decline and inequality to rise.

Estimates show that the cost of corruption equals more than 5% of global GDP, or USD 2.6 trillion (World Economic Forum), with over USD 1 trillion paid in bribes each year (World Bank). The costs of corruption can be felt in many different ways.

Because they are less adept at estimating the likelihood of danger or return on their investment, investors frequently avoid investing in nations where systems are thought to be corrupt.

The introduction of measures to detect and combat corruption as well as corrupt officials both have the potential to slow down bureaucratic procedures. Additionally, there may be connections between corruption and other illegal activities including tax evasion, money laundering, and major organized crime.

Bribery is the deliberate offering, promise, or provision of an improper financial or other advantage to an official or decision-maker with the intent to influence their actions or inaction in connection with the execution of their duties.

In any business-related bribery transaction there are four main parties: the briber; the bribed person and their respective organizations.

These organizations are occasionally, though not always, the direct victims of bribery. For instance, a government agency may overpay for services as part of a kickback scheme, or a private company may enter into contracts with unfavorable terms as a result of the actions of the briber and the bribed person.

There may also be many indirect victims of bribery, including individuals who suffer when funds are diverted from public services and law-abiding businesses that miss out on contracts because they refuse to pay bribes.

1.3.4. Tax Evasion

Tax evasion is a criminal offense in which an individual or a business knowingly fails to pay their actual tax obligations. Tax evasion is typically punishable by criminal prosecution and severe fines. The Internal Revenue Service (IRS) tax code defines willful tax evasion as a federal crime.

Tax evasion encompasses both the unlawful non-payment of taxes and the unlawful underpayment of taxes. Even if a taxpayer fails to submit appropriate tax forms, the IRS can still determine if taxes were owed based on the information required to be sent in by third parties, such as W-2 information from a person's employer or 1099s. A person is typically not judged to be guilty of tax evasion unless the failure to pay is thought to be deliberate.

Failure to pay proper taxes can lead to criminal charges. It must be established that the taxpayer's attempt to avoid paying taxes was a deliberate decision before charges can be brought. In addition to being responsible for paying any unpaid taxes, a person may also be found guilty of official charges and sentenced to jail time.

According to the IRS, the penalties include jail time of no more than five years, a fine of no more than $2,50,000 for individuals or $5,00,000 for corporations, or both—along with the costs of prosecution.

A number of variables are considered when deciding whether the act of failure to pay was intentional. Most frequently, a taxpayer's financial status will be investigated to see whether the non-payment was due to fraud or the concealing of reportable income.

If a taxpayer attempted to conceal assets by tying them to someone other than themselves, the refusal to pay may be deemed to be dishonest.

This can include reporting income under a false name and social security number (SSN), which can also constitute identity theft. If work that did not adhere to conventional payment recording techniques was not reported, the person could be accused of concealing revenue. Accepting monetary payment for products or services supplied without properly disclosing them to the IRS during tax filing is one example of this.

1.3.5. Embezzlement

A purposeful misappropriation of the funds entrusted to someone, or something is referred to as embezzlement, which is a type of white-collar crime. In this kind of fraud, the embezzler obtains the funds legitimately and is entitled to possess them, but the assets are then used for unanticipated objectives.

Embezzlement is a breach of the fiduciary responsibilities placed upon a person. Anyone granted access to an organization's funds is under obligation to keep those resources secure for that purpose. To knowingly take that money and utilize it for personal gain is against the law. Diverting cash to accounts that seem to be authorized to receive payments or transfers is one example of such activity.

The account, though, is merely a cover through which the person might accept the money – or it can be taken by a partner organization. For instance, to make the transfer of money appear to be a legal transaction, an embezzler may manufacture invoices and receipts for services or commercial transactions that never occurred. An embezzler may work with a partner who is designated as a consultant or contractor but never actually provides the services they are billing for. This partner may generate bills and collect payment. The nature of embezzlement can be both small and large. Embezzling funds can be as minor as a store clerk pocketing a few bucks from a cash register.

On a larger scale, however, embezzlement also happens when high-ranking business leaders falsely claim millions of dollars in expenses and transfer the money into personal accounts. Depending on the severity of the offense, embezzlement may result in steep penalties and lengthy prison sentences.

Theft and embezzlement cost companies approximately $400 billion per year and account for more than 50% of business failures (Figure 1.4).

Figure 1.4. A word cloud featuring "Embezzlement."

Source: Image by Flickr.

However, employers can develop strategies to combat these white-collar crimes. The first step in embezzlement is the betrayal of confidence by a person who has wasgiven the responsibility to look after another person's property or finances. Considerably, properly screening potential hires is one of the first actions a company may take. Assessing character qualities via personality tests could identify problematic behaviors in addition to doing full background investigations.

Corporate crime may be discouraged by a security and surveillance program, particularly if it is conducted by a committed risk management team or an impartial third party. These risk managers can design internal checks that keep an eye on actions, enable anonymous reporting of suspicious activity, and carry out recurring audits that reveal theft.

Early detection helps to mitigate losses and protect the company's reputation and the people it serves. Employers should be transparent about their zero-tolerance approach toward unlawful behaviors like embezzlement and explain the repercussions of such violations. Every business should foster an environment of justice and honesty and should encourage staff members to be watchful and report instances of misconduct.

1.4. ACTIVITIES AND EXTENT OF FINANCIAL CRIME

1.4.1. Activities

Examples of financial crime are money-laundering, tax evasion, fraud (embezzlement, check, and credit card fraud, securities fraud, insurance fraud, health care fraud and pension fraud), stock manipulation, tax avoidance, bribery, and corruption, insider trading, terrorist financing, etc. FBI (2005) focuses its investigations on corporate fraud, health care fraud, mortgage fraud, identity theft, insurance fraud, and money laundering.

The usage of networks like the internet allows financial crime to be typically international, according to Interpol. Transnational crime and cybercrime are intrinsically linked to financial crime, having a negative effect on financial institutions or people all over the world. Why is financial crime more likely to be transnational and hinge on electronic networks?

It is first necessary to store the proceeds of financial crime in a secure location that local law enforcement cannot find. By doing so, the likelihood of being caught is decreased when the proceeds are sent to countries where cross-border cooperation is less effective.

In addition, wiring the revenues avoids the need for customs inspections, which restricts the reach of law enforcement. Because internet money transactions are instantaneous, it is impossible for local officials to identify and seize the revenues before they are transferred outside of the country.

These tendencies line up with Castells' (2000) list of informational, global, and networked society traits. Let's consider the remittance of unlawful funds. It can be elaborated that "financial information on the proceeds is delivered to a third person beyond the border (global) via computer networks." This justification supports the claim that financial crime accurately represents the contemporary societal shift to an information age.

1.4.2. Extent

It seems to be impossible to accurately calculate the extent of financial crime (Ryder, 2001). A study from the UNODC (2011) estimated that in 2009 all criminal proceeds were likely to amount to 3.6% of global GDP, which was equivalent to about $2.1 trillion.

Besides, the research pointed out that the volume of international money-laundering was expected to be about 2.7% of global GDP or $1.6 trillion. The IMF recommended a "consensus range" for money laundering in 1998, which is between 2% and 5% of global GDP. This money laundering number falls within this range.

This estimate would be translated into from $590 billion to $1.5 trillion by using actual numbers of 1998, while FATF estimated about $500 billion. The lower figure roughly equates to the value of the total output of an economy the size of Spain.

In terms of corruption which is "abuse of entrusted power for private gain" (Transparency International), the World Bank states that approximately $1 trillion is paid in bribes around the world.

Considering the economic and societal ripple effects, the World Economic Forum estimates that the cost of corruption equates to 5% of global GDP, which is about $2.6 trillion, and that corruption increases the cost of doing business by up to 10% on average (World Economic Journal).

According to IMF data, investment in corrupt countries is around 5% lower than it is in relatively corrupt countries (OECD, 2013). It is crucial to note that corruption has a negative impact on a nation's capital productivity (Lambsdorff, 2003).

The justification for combating corruptive behavior is strengthened by the claim that corruption is strongly linked to economic development in a nation.

The UNODC estimated that in the U.S. about $300 billion or about 2% of the economy was generated in illicit proceeds in 2010. Among all the financial crimes in the US, illicit drug sales and fraud was estimated to account for most proceeds.

The UK HM Treasury (2007) estimated that over £20 billion of social and economic damage was brought about in the UK and more than half of the damage is generated by illicit drug use. KPMG's 2012 survey with 281 respondents reported that the total value of fraud for public and private sector organizations in Australia and New Zealand was $372.7 million, with an average loss per organization of $3.08 million. According to the Australian Institute of Criminology (2011), fraud is estimated to have cost the Australian society $6.05 billion in 2011. In conclusion, these data indicate that key illicit activities that cause harm on a national and worldwide level include fraud, drug sales, and money laundering.

1.5. VICTIMS OF FINANCIAL CRIME

All spheres of society are affected by victims, who range from individuals to institutions and companies (Gottschalk, 2010). Serious financial crimes have an impact on both organizations and ordinary persons at the micro-level.

Many people lost their assets and security as a result of some market frauds, which also had an adverse impact on their relationships, physical health, emotional health, and security (Australian Crime Commission).

Through the significant financial losses sustained, financial crime has a detrimental effect on the entire economic and social system on a macro-level:

- **Individual internal Victims:** Individuals in the organization are the victims.
- **Individual External Victims:** Individuals outside the organization are the victims.
- **Organizational Internal Victims:** Organizations as such are the victims.
- **Organizational External Victims:** Outside organizations are the victims.

Varying types of victims have different stakes in various types of financial crime. First off, individuals who use financial institution services frequently become victims of insider or outsider fraud and identity theft.

The Ponzi scheme by Bernard Madoff in 2008 is an example of fraud by an insider and it can also be called occupational financial crime. Due to increased internal control, insider fraud is less likely to occur, but when it does, the harm is severe.

Instead, criminals who do not work for a financial institution tend to target people more often. Phishing is becoming the most common form of fraud against people, which is pretty evident. Criminals can utilize computers and networks to send automated calls, emails, or text messages to tens of thousands of potential victims. As cyber financial crime, phishing affects everyone with a relatively small amount of damage, but large in aggregate.

Second, companies, particularly financial institutions, become victims of financial crime. While customers and other outside parties may be liable for identity fraud, insurance fraud, consumer fraud, and other crimes, insiders are more likely to conduct crimes including corruption, embezzlement, cash, and inventory theft, and intellectual property theft.

Thirdly, financial crime undermines the stability of national economies (FATF). According to Ryder (2011), financial crime's repercussions can jeopardize national security by eroding the credibility of a country's financial institutions. The Enron crisis was the major incident that severely impacted the US economy. In fact, there are times when a national financial scandal has an impact on the entire global economy.

Finally, victims on a global scale include the institutions and international financial system. Combating money laundering and the financing of terrorists has received considerable importance in Western countries. Responding to calls from the international community, international organizations such as IMF and FATF have extended their reach to the areas of AML and combating the financing of terrorism (CFT).

The protection of the global financial system's integrity is their primary goal. This year, it was revealed that organizations associated with international sport, including FIFA and the IAAF, have significant internal financial issues, which is corruption.

Choosing the World Cup host cities and hiding the results of positive doping tests were the topics of the scandals involving FIFA and IAAF, respectively. It is very baffling that non-profit organizations tasked with upholding a high standard of integrity struggle to prevent kickbacks and bribes. However, it is not easy to pinpoint victims on a global scale for two reasons. First, victims such as the financial system are intangibles. Second, the actual amount of financial damage is intricate to figure out.

1.6. THE FACILITATING FACTORS AND PRIORITIES OF PUBLIC INSTITUTIONS

1.6.1. Facilitating Factors

According to IMF (2001), financial abuse is a result of globalization and the integration of the financial markets. It suggests that the degree of global interconnectedness is inversely correlated with the size and severity of financial crime.

According to the Australian Crime Commission, technology, globalization, and market diversification are the main causes of this kind of crime. There is a belief that tax haven networks facilitate international financial crime.

The financial secrecy of some jurisdictions such as Switzerland and the Cayman Islands provides the favorable environment for fraud, market manipulation, and money laundering (Ruggiero, 2015).

Others took a criminological approach to tackling financial crime. According to Michel (2008), opportunity drives financial crime, therefore it is important to deal with opportunistic bad actors like procedural flaws.

This claim is mostly supported by the rational choice theory. If they believe that the benefits of financial crime outweigh the costs of doing it and getting caught, the risk will be worthwhile. Either reducing costs or increasing benefits will lead to a higher return of investment (ROI).

This viewpoint has something to do with the justifications for tax fraud and money laundering. The likelihood of financial crime increasing is higher if the assured deposit of illegal earnings in a secure location.

1.6.2. Priorities of Public Institutions

While FATF and IMF's primary initiatives center on money laundering and terrorism financing, Interpol devotes the majority of its resources to combating money laundering, the use of counterfeit money and security papers, payment card fraud, lottery fraud, and Nigerian letter scams. Additionally, the World Bank and OECD are serious about corruption (Figure 1.5).

International organizations try to stop extensive illegal activity carried out by organized crime gangs. Each nation has its own efforts to combat financial crime at the national level.

After the 2008 financial crisis brought on by deficiencies in financial regulation and fraudulent financial products, the US has been addressing fraud, money laundering, and counterfeit currency seriously and is focusing more on corporate fraud, market manipulation fraud, and mortgage fraud.

The National Crime Agency in the UK directly deals with money laundering and counterfeit currency, cooperating with Serious Fraud Office (SFO) when it comes to fraud, bribery, and corruption.

Figure 1.5. OECD global anti-corruption and integrity forum.

Source: Image by Flickr.

To preserve the integrity and order of international financial markets, there is general agreement among some of the top international and national bodies that fighting corruption, fraud, money laundering, and counterfeit money should be their top objectives.

Similarly, common themes are also found on the national level, which are health care fraud, insurance fraud, identity theft, intellectual property theft, etc.

1.7. RELATIONSHIPS AMONG FINANCIAL CRIMES

Financial and non-financial crimes can both occur independently, although some financial crimes may also entail other crimes. Australian Crime Commission reports that key crime enablers include money laundering, cyber, and technology-enabled crime, identity crime, exploitation of business structures, and public sector corruption. These are frequently illegal actions in and of themselves that serve as a catalyst for other forms of organized crime.

1.7.1. Money Laundering

FATF defines it as "the processing of criminal proceeds to disguise their illegal origin," while the U.S. Treasury department explains it in greater detail as "financial transactions that criminals, including terrorist organizations, attempt to disguise the proceeds, sources or nature of their illegal activities." Prior to pursuing money laundering, there should be a predicate offense. Therefore, it is not considered money laundering if the funds are not identified as being the proceeds of crime. Physical crimes can be the predicate crime, but according to IMF (2001), financial crimes are more frequently the culprit.

According to a country's environment and jurisdiction, different predicate crime types exist. Most financial crimes are said to involve money-laundering, according to the broad consensus, to avoid being reported by law authorities.

1.7.2. Identity Theft

Identity theft is generally committed to facilitate other crimes, such as credit card fraud, check fraud or mortgage fraud, and phishing. Based on data from an identity theft, fraudsters invent a tale or function as someone else to con potential victims. Identity theft, according to Gottschalk (2010), helps identity fraud happen.

1.7.3. Exploitation of Business Structures

Multiple offshore countries can be used to conceal real beneficiaries in complex company structures and sophisticated networks of corporations. Money laundering, tax fraud, the sale of illicit goods, investment fraud, and fraud with retirement funds are the main components of this technique.

Global corporations, notably financial institutions, frequently use this technique to avoid paying corporate tax or siphon off illegal funds.

1.7.4. Public Sector Corruption

Organized criminal groups attempt to corrupt politicians or public officials in an effort to gain access to information, public funds and to affect future investigations on them. Drug trafficking and people trafficking are two examples of non-financial crimes that are facilitated by this facilitator. For instance, accepting bribes invariably results in money laundering and tax evasion.

1.7.5. Relationships with Cybercrime

The internet may serve as a fertile ground for financial crimes (Wall, 2007). The association between cybercrime and several financial crimes is well documented. The majority of financial crimes committed nowadays technically fall under the category of "cyber-enabled crime" because the offenders eventually use networked ICTs (information and communications technology) to their benefit while committing the crime.

Similarly, to cybercrimes, financial crimes are made more widespread and of a larger scale by the usage of networked computers and other ICTs. McGuire & Dowling (2013) posit that fraud and theft are the most widely published instances of cyber-enabled crime.

Main forms of cyber-enabled fraud are electronic financial frauds (internet banking fraud), fraudulent sales through online or retail sites, mass-marketing frauds, consumer scams, phishing, and online romance. According to Snyder & Crescenzi (2009), cybercrime, and intellectual property crime are related, and the rise in cybercrime opens the door for more businesses' intellectual property to be targeted.

1.8. TOP SIX BIGGEST FINANCIAL CRIMES

1.8.1. Bernard (Bernie) Madoff

Bernard Madoff was an investment advisor and financier (someone who manages large amounts of money on behalf of large organizations, governments, etc.). However, Madoff is most recognized for operating the biggest Ponzi scheme in the annals of financial crime.

Madoff actively convinced people to invest with him by explaining his "low-risk" investment strategy called a "split-strike conversion" (sometimes referred to as a 'collar') which is used to avoid high losses in the market. On these investments, he guaranteed large profits. In actuality, they were fabricating trading records and compensating early investors with fresh capital.

It's possible that from the time it was created in the 1970s until the early 2000s, this remained mostly unreported. An investigation into financial fraud and forensic accounting by Harry Markopolos revealed evidence that suggested Bernie Madoff's wealth management company was merely a massive Ponzi scam.

Markopolos noted that Madoff's calculations indicated that in order to deliver the returns he was promised, they would need to be purchasing more than was offered on the market. Despite this, Madoff didn't confess to his scam until he was hauled into the FBI by his sons in 2008 when he didn't have the money to make the necessary pay-outs. Approximately $65 billion USD was reported missing from his client's accounts. In 2009, he was sentenced to 150 years in prison for his many counts of fraud and was banned from trading. In February 2020, he filed for compassionate release due to kidney failure.

1.8.2. Samuel Israel III

Samuel Israel III is a former CEO and hedge fund manager. Israel raised $450 million from investors only to later misappropriate these funds for his own personal use.

Israel was utilizing the funds from these investors to fund a Ponzi scheme. His company established a fictitious accounting firm to "fact check" their data and keep up the idea that they were conducting business honestly after a year with extraordinarily low returns.

In 2005, his scheme was revealed, and he was indicted being sentenced to 20 years in prison for his crimes (in 2008).

However, that is not all. In contrast to Bernie Madoff, who was planning to turn himself in when he admitted his crimes, Israel left after receiving his sentence. The words "Suicide is Painless" had been scratched in the dirt onto the hood of his abandoned car. Debra Ryan, Israel's girlfriend, acknowledged assisting in his escape. They both appeared on America's Most Wanted in a well-known episode.

Later in 2008, he was found in Massachusetts and his sentence was extended by two years for his attempt to flee.

1.8.3. Tom Petters

Tom Petters' resume of financial crimes includes the following: conspiracy, mail fraud, wire fraud, and money laundering, among others. Het was described by one of his associates as essentially a giant, elaborate Ponzi scheme.

False bank statements were used by Petters and associates to entice investors to invest with them (under the operational name Petters Group Worldwide). They would subsequently secure bank loans totaling billions of dollars using the acquired and invested funds in order to pay off prior loans.

When lenders wired money to large box stores, the stores would then pay the money on to Petters (and others), minus a "commission," using fabricated paperwork to claim they were buying goods from the establishments.

The money was utilized to compensate scheme participants, Petters' other businesses, and Petters himself to support an extravagant lifestyle.

With a reliable informant, the FBI started looking into Petters in 2008 for proof of the loan and investment scam based on fictitious transactions as well as tax fraud.

He was eventually convicted of these federal crimes for operating Petters Group Worldwide as a $3.65 billion Ponzi scheme and sentenced to serve 50 years in prison. Even with all the evidence against him and his criminal conviction, he still pleads he is innocent.

1.8.4. Allen Stanford

Allen Stanford was a financier running yet another massive Ponzi scheme. His scheme extended beyond U.S. borders to also include banks in the Caribbean and within Venezuela.

Topersuade potential investors to join with him, Stanford portrayed hypothetical profits as genuine business data and asserted that his certificates of deposits (CDs) were safer than accounts insured by the US government.

By altering Stanford International Banks documents, he was able to conceal their plot while misappropriating money. In 2009, he was charged by the Securities and Exchange Commission (SEC) for a whopping $8 billion investment scheme.

After trying to flee the country, his accounts being frozen, arrested, claiming medical problems and being unfit to stand trial, a judge finally found him fit for trial in 2011. After a 2012 trial, he was found guilty and given a 110-year prison term for designing and conducting one of the biggest Ponzi Schemes ever.

1.8.5. Scott W. Rothstein

Scott W. Rothstein is a disbarred lawyer and the former managing shareholder, chairman, and chief executive officer of Rothstein Rosenfeldt Adler law firm.

Rothstein's Ponzi scheme was riddled with "highly confidential" legal settlements. In the simplest terms, Rothstein gave investors the possibility to "buy" significant litigation settlements at discounted rates, so granting them the right to payments with higher profits.

That was undoubtedly not the case, though. Investors were anticipating significant returns on their investments and allegedly already got settlement money from the defendants. Rothstein was not alone in exploiting these investor funds to support his extravagant lifestyle; the other lawyers at the firm were as well. For a few years, this went on, until in 2009, money ran out to pay investors, and Rothstein left the country.

He returned to the nation a short while later and handed himself in. After helping the authorities with their investigation, he eventually entered a guilty plea. He received prison time along with many of his friends and family, including his wife.

He is currently serving a 50-year prison sentence (in an undisclosed location) for running a $1.2 billion Ponzi scheme.

1.8.6. Marc Dreier

Last but certainly not least, there is the case of Marc Dreier. Dreier is yet another ex-attorney who still practices law out of his office in New York. He was the brains behind a Ponzi scheme that defrauded investors by offering them phony financial instruments, assets, or packages of assets that could be traded.

Dreier set up meetings with financiers and individuals posing as US and Canadian government representatives to offer the fake promissory notes. He continued doing this to the tune of $700 million USD.

He was initially detained for attempting to sell financial products while within Canada while posing as an attorney. After being granted bail and returning to the US, he was promptly detained once more for his ongoing Ponzi scheme.

Dreier was eventually disbarred by the New York Supreme Court in 2009 and was sentenced to 20 years in prison for 8 counts of fraud. He is scheduled to be released in 2026, a few years earlier than the original sentence.

1.9. MEASURES AGAINST FINANCIAL CRIMES

There are many national and global organizations to combat financial crimes. For instance, the US and Treasury Department's FinCEN office gathers and examines financial transactions in order to prevent both domestic and foreign money laundering, terrorist funding, and other financial crimes.

Companies must abide by the rules that these organizations publish. Organizations that don't follow the rules are subject to penalties from the regulators. Financial institutions must comply with compliance regulations such as AML and know your customer (KYC) requirements. With the development of technology, methods of combating financial crimes are developing.

Solutions for preventing financial crimes have risen in recent years due to the growing RegTech industry. The detection and prevention of financial crimes are made possible by AML solutions created using AI and machine learning techniques. Because manual control methods are ineffective and consume a lot of time, AML solutions are growing in popularity year after year.

Solutions from Sanction Scanner assist businesses in preventing financial crimes and adhering to AML rules. During the customer onboarding and customer monitoring processes, AML Name Screening Software enables businesses to manage their customers' exposure to sanctions, PEP, and negative media material.

Financial institutions can regulate the source and recipient of money transfer transactions when sanction, PEP, and negative media data are present by using transaction screening software. AML Transaction Monitoring Software, on the other hand, makes certain that all transactions from all clients are automatically managed in accordance with risk criteria and scenarios and that anomalous transactions are discovered.

International as well as national authorities attempt to battle financial crime through research and legislation, which mandates specific types of organizations, such as banks, estate agents and iGaming companies, to know who they are dealing with. It also holds them accountable for allowing financial crime to be perpetrated on their platforms.

On the companies' side, strategies, solutions, and individual tools to combat economic crime abound, and tend to belong to several distinct categories:

- **KYC and Onboarding Tools:** When a customer first signs up for an account or product with a financial organization, the latter is mandated to run tests to confirm the customer's identity. This is called the KYC step and is assisted by specialized software.
- **Identity Verification Software (IDV):** This form of preventative measure, known as IDV for short, tries to confirm the customer's identity manually or automatically by evaluating the reliability of the proof they provided during KYC. This can be done online through a video chat with an expert or algorithms that look into things like scanned passports and the like.

- **Transaction Monitoring and AML Software:** Banks and neo-banks are required to do due diligence on their clients in accordance with AML regulations. Part of this is monitoring their transactions for any over a set minimum amount (e.g., $3,000 in the US), as well as other Due Diligence (CDD) and enhanced due diligence (EDD) measures, which change from country to country.
- **End-to-End Risk/Fraud Prevention:** Fighting financial fraud can be aided by software designed to spot and prevent fraudulent behavior. This can be used independently or as a component of a larger risk stack, depending on its characteristics and the complexity of the environment where it is deployed.
- **Authentication Protocols:** Financial companies use robust authentication systems to prevent account takeover attacks (ATOs), which would allow the attacker to commit financial fraud and crimes against the economy. These verify that the person checking in is the rightful account owner and may use biometrics like voice and fingerprint recognition, two-factor authentication, etc.
- **Compliance Suites:** This kind of solution will take care of an organization's regulatory requirements and worries, lowering the possibility of costly fines and enabling trouble-free operation in various locations.
- **Risk Monitoring:** It is a continuous process where businesses at high risk of being attacked or unwittingly aiding in economic crimes monitor and analyze their risk prevention tactics as they proceed. It is more of a framework than a single technology.

1.10. FINANCIAL CRIME RISK MANAGEMENT

Risk management for financial crime is the proactive pursuit of financial crime detection and prevention. To lessen the effects of financial crime, it is done through spotting suspicious activities and weaknesses that an organization possess.

Several tools, such as hiring analysts or creating software to prevent financial crime, can help with risk management for financial crime. Overall, all stakeholders work together to prevent and mitigate financial crime, and this results in financial crime risk management.

1.10.1. The Current State of Financial Crime Risk Management

Ever since money first became a means of transaction, there has been financial crime. Cash or other financial assets may have been physically stolen by thieves in the past. Electronic payments and bank accounts increasingly predominate our financial architecture thanks to technological advancements. In order to commit financial crimes, criminals have thus become more and more dependent on technology.

Cybercriminals are those who commit crimes by attacking people or organizations using technology. These fraudsters have used a variety of crafty and sophisticated techniques to obtain financial data without leaving a trace. Cybercriminals may be external, sitting outside of an organization. However, they can also come from inside an organization.

No matter where the organization is located or what industry it operates in, these crimes can happen anywhere. These offenses are also perpetrated against specific people. The importance of having preventative risk management procedures in place increases as more data moves online.

1.11. REDUCING FINANCIAL CRIME RISK IN ORGANIZATIONS

The laws set the precedent for how your organization can prevent and address financial crimes within the organization. Knowing which rules apply to you, monitoring changes in the laws, and building awareness about them across the organization are your top priorities.

These best practices will also help you prevent criminal activity:

- **Start at the Top:** All stakeholders, from frontline staff to the C-suite, must be on board for FCRM strategies to be successful, and executives must be actively involved in the process. Executives should have access to intelligence reports that give a clear picture of how the company is managing risks, and security staff should meet with business leaders frequently to discuss pain points and weaknesses.
- **Assign Clear Responsibilities and Roles:** Give staff members many opportunities to report any suspicious activity, and make sure individuals in charge of seeing and dealing with financial crime concerns are well trained. All staff members should receive training on the company's FCRM rules, how they relate to their

individual roles within the company, and how to recognize criminal activities.

- **Create Cross-Departmental Teams:** IT plays a huge role in financial crime prevention, as do legal and compliance teams, but you should also include employees from customer service, HR, sales, accounting, business development and other groups, especially as you examine all possible risk scenarios.
- **Review Third-Party Vendors:** Make sure the suppliers you work with adhere to the same rules as your business to avoid any potential liability.
- **Support Your Financial Crime and AML Analysts with Technology:** Invest in fraud detection, AML solutions and security automation, among other solutions. Your analysts will be better able to concentrate on genuine threats and compliance-related tasks if they spend less time on dead ends, false positives, and repeated chores.

1.12. THE FUTURE OF FIGHTING FINANCIAL CRIME

To safeguard their clients, themselves, and their reputations from loss and harm, financial institutions must stay on top of developing fraud trends and regulatory compliance issues.

To combat financial crime and increase compliance, institutions should take into account end-to-end financial crime management solutions that include real-time fraud detection, targeted AML transaction monitoring, and automated regulatory reporting.

Behavior-based anti-financial crime management solutions can assist institutions in improving the effectiveness and efficiency of their fraud and AML programs by utilizing artificial intelligence, including machine learning and robotic process automation (RPA).

But artificial intelligence relies on the power of big data. Anti-financial crime management solutions need an immense data set from multiple sources, including core, ancillary, open-source, and third-party and consortium data.

In a cloud-based setting, cross-institutional analysis of this data can be done using artificial intelligence. Big data and AI-based solutions improve the quality and accuracy of warnings while decreasing false positives.

Machine learning-based analytical agents continually study data to enhance analytical performance. Machine learning agents can train on labeled data from hundreds of institutions using a big, cross-institutional data set in a cloud-based environment, achieving performance levels that are unattainable for a single university using a small, isolated, and constrained data set.

Machine learning may enhance analytical performance, assisting organizations in lowering false positives and shortening the time spent reviewing alerts to improve the effectiveness of investigations while continuing to identify new and developing criminal tendencies.

Machine learning agents use mathematical and statistical models to learn from data without being explicitly programmed. These agents analyze new data, including transactions, demographics, and customer behavior, and utilize this evidence in transaction monitoring alerts.

The alerts provide feedback to the cloud-based data set, where the training data, which includes the transaction, demographic, and customer-behavior evidence, and labeled data, such as cases, marked transactions and return items, are inputted to a machine learning algorithm.

This information is utilized to train a variety of machine learning agents in order to ascertain which agent performs the best for a given typology. To provide an unbiased validation of the training outcomes, the data is divided into training, testing, and validation data sets before training an agent.

Anti-financial crime management solutions can use precision, recall, and false positive rate to validate analytical performance and assign the most suitable analytical agent to a particular fraud or money laundering typology.

1.12.1. Strengthening Processes with Robotic Process Automation (RPA)

Institutions can leverage technology such as RPA to improve internal processes, strengthen anti-financial crime management programs and ensure regulatory compliance.

Financial crime investigators can save time by decreasing manual duties, automating stages in alert triage and regulatory reporting processes, and pre-populating and submitting reports with consistency, speed, and accuracy by using RPA to increase workflow automation.

RPA-enhanced data collecting lowers human error that happens during manual data transfer and gathering. Additionally, it combines various data sources automatically and dependably into your anti-financial crime management and compliance systems. Anti-financial crime management programs can use RPA agents to validate information populated in a currency transaction report or a SAR, automatically submit reports, intelligently package related alerts together, and automatically assign work to a team or an investigator.

Such solutions can also automatically triage alerts and segment customers into appropriate risk categories, increasing the efficiency and effectiveness of financial crime investigations.

Financial institutions should think about the advantages of cloud-based solutions that use artificial intelligence to boost the efficacy and efficiency of anti-financial crime management and compliance programs in order to remain ahead of financial crime trends.

1.13. CONCLUSION

Financial criminality is discussed in this chapter. This chapter's introduction clarifies the categories of financial crimes as well as who can commit them. The actions and scope of financial crime, as well as its victims, are highlighted in this chapter as well. Also mentioned are the public institutions' enabling elements and top priorities.

In the middle of this chapter, we discuss the six biggest financial crimes and measures against financial crimes have been discussed. This chapter also addresses risk management for financial crime. The future of the fight against financial crime has been covered toward the end of this chapter, as has lowering the risk of financial crime in organizations.

REFERENCES

1. Chen, J., (2022). *Money Laundering: What it is and How to Prevent it*. Investopedia. Available at: https://www.investopedia.com/terms/m/moneylaundering.asp (accessed on 15 June 2023).
2. *Financial Crime,* (2022). WallStreetMojo. Available at: https://www.wallstreetmojo.com/financial-crime/ (accessed on 15 June 2023).
3. Hayes, A., (2022). *What is Embezzlement, and How Does it Happen?* Investopedia. Available at: https://www.investopedia.com/terms/e/embezzlement.asp (accessed on 15 June 2023).
4. Jung, J., & Lee, J., (n.d.). *Contemporary Financial Crime, Journal of Public Administration and Governance*. Available at: https://doi.org/10.5296/jpag.v7i2.11219 (accessed on 15 June 2023).
5. Kagan, J., (2022). *Tax Evasion: Meaning, Definition, and Penalties*. Investopedia. Available at: https://www.investopedia.com/terms/t/taxevasion.asp (accessed on 15 June 2023).
6. *Terrorist Financing,* (n.d.). United Nations: Office on Drugs and Crime. Available at: https://www.unodc.org/unodc/en/terrorism/news-and-events/terrorist-financing.html (accessed on 15 June 2023).
7. *Types of Financial Crime: Definition, Examples & Trends,* (2022). SEON. Available at: https://seon.io/resources/financial-crimes/ (accessed on 15 June 2023).
8. *What is Financial Crime?* (n.d.). sanctionscanner.com. Sanction scanner. Available at: https://sanctionscanner.com/blog/what-is-financial-crime-9#:~:text=Financial%20Crimes%20are%20criminal%20activities,to%20the%20economy%20and%20society (accessed on 15 June 2023).
9. *What is Money Laundering? Definition of Money Laundering and Money Laundering Meaning,* (n.d.). The Economic Times. Available at: https://economictimes.indiatimes.com/definition/money-laundering (accessed on 15 June 2023).
10. *Who Commits Financial Crime?* (2023). Financial Crime Academy. Available at: https://financialcrimeacademy.org/who-commits-financial-crime/ (accessed on 15 June 2023).

CHAPTER 2

Risk, Recklessness, and Policing the Financial Markets

Contents

This chapter explains about the risk, recklessness, and policing the financial markets. The beginning of the chapter explains about reckless risk taking, securitization, and the global financial crisis (GFC), reckless risk taking and dishonesty. The chapter also addresses the innovative approach to fight crime towards standard setting. The chapter provides the highlights on the financial intelligence units (FIUs), common challenges in developing countries. The end of the chapter explains the automation, bioethics, accountability, and policing.

2.1. INTRODUCTION

Lanny Breuer, an assistant attorney general in the US Department of Justice (DOJ), is reported as saying in a Financial Times article titled "US housing: After the Gold Rush" on October 29, 2012 that "the securitization cases at the corporate level are challenging because the things that are so disheartening and contributed to the financial crisis are not activities which violated the criminal law." (Need a page number here)

According to a widespread belief, the obstacle to criminal prosecution is the difficulty of establishing that players in the financial market acted dishonestly, which is the hallmark of criminal intent.

The global financial crisis (GFC) has undoubtedly resulted in a wide range of civil settlements, but criminal prosecutions have been uncommon. It is accurate to state that the criminal law has not really addressed the current GFC at all.

As Charles Ferguson, the renowned film director who produced Inside Job, a feature length documentary about the GFC, indicated when accepting his winning nomination at the Oscars ceremony in Los Angeles on 27 February 2011, "I must start by pointing out that three years after our horrific financial crisis caused by massive fraud, not a single financial executive has gone to jail, and that's wrong."

In saying this, Mr. Ferguson was merely reflecting the sentiment of the general public, whose forbearance has been worn thin by the discovery of widespread financial misconduct.

On 9th October 2012 the Evening Standard published details of a public opinion survey conducted by YouGov on behalf of Avaaz, a global non-government campaigning organization, which revealed that 89% of a sampled group in the UK wanted sentences of imprisonment for bankers who manipulated the financial markets.

When thinking about criminal responsibility for reckless risk-taking, the wording employed by Alex Wilks, the campaign director for Avaaz, when releasing the poll's findings, is very pertinent. Mr. Wilks stated that because "bankers are enormously rewarded for their risky bets and get off much too lightly when caught," people throughout Europe want to see bankers put behind bars (Figure 2.1).

Figure 2.1. Mr. Charles Ferguson, the renowned film director who produced Inside Job.

Source: Image by Flickr.

Writing in the Financial Times on the 22nd May 2013, John Kay, a highly respected economic commentator, expressed the position more bluntly: "The financial crisis left a few individuals responsible for it very rich while its consequences made many millions not responsible for it much poorer. If this involves no crime, then we have failed to define or prosecute crime appropriately."

The objective of this chapter is to show that the widely held belief that the criminal justice system is ineffective is false. There were numerous examples of apparent carelessness that the criminal law should have been able to appropriately prosecute in the securitization cases and other cases of egregious misbehavior in connection with the financial markets.

Criminal justice theory dictates that it be done because not only are the parameters of the criminal law broad enough to penalize instances of irresponsible behavior by participants in the financial markets where they cause harm to others. The case for criminal responsibility for reckless risk-taking on the financial markets is a strong one, as the United Kingdom

Parliament has recently recognized with the creation of a new criminal offense of taking a risk which causes a bank to fail contrary to Section 29 of the Financial Services (Banking Reform) Act 2013.

A more general question about whether excessive risk-taking on the financial markets should also be criminalized where consumer interests are negatively impacted is raised by the passage of a clause that is only applicable to bank failures.

2.2. RECKLESSNESS RISK-TAKING, SECURITIZATION, AND THE GLOBAL FINANCIAL CRISIS (GFC)

In regard to the securitization cases that Mr. Breuer mentioned, it is challenging to know where to begin with any illustration of the magnitude of careless risk-taking on the financial markets that contributed to the global crisis' onset.

Financial journalist and non-fiction author Michael Lewis makes an argument that significant issues were brought by senior management in investment banks in some cases being so careless they were not even aware of the risks they were running in his sober but somewhat amusing review of the GFC.

In layman's terms, securitization is the financial practice of pooling various types of contractual debt, such as residential mortgages, commercial mortgages, car loans, or credit card debt obligations, and selling the pooled debt on the financial markets as investments to investors.

The investors who acquired the pooled product are subsequently paid with the money obtained from the underlying debt, along with interest and revenues from the debt repayment. In this approach, it is possible to say that the revenue came from the pooled product, also known as a derivative investment or just a derivative and included in the category of financial instruments.

But a derivative investment is a wide term and it can also include a variety of financial contracts, including contracts involving the purchase or sale of shares and here the terminology becomes almost impenetrable as references are made to contracts for futures, forwards, swaps, options, and variations of these contractual arrangements involving caps, floors, collars, and credit default swaps which are often known by their acronym "CDS."

Even though it can be challenging to understand, a CDS is a financial swap agreement whereby the seller of the CDS, who is the owner of a financial instrument made up of a number of pooled loans, promises to pay the buyer in the event of a loan failure or other credit event.

The buyer of the CDS makes a series of payments known as the CDS "fee" or "spread" to the seller and, in exchange, receives a compensatory payment if the loan defaults.

2.3. RECKLESS RISK-TAKING AND DISHONESTY

2.3.1. Dishonesty

Legal professionals and academic lawyers agree that taking reckless risks on the financial markets does not constitute engaging in fraudulent activity because dishonesty is the litmus test for fraudulent behavior and reckless behavior, however repugnant it may be, falls short of dishonesty. This, of course, begs the critical question as to what is meant by the word "dishonest."

The Oxford English Dictionary defines a dishonest person as somebody who is "behaving or prone to behave in an untrustworthy, deceitful, or insincere way," and a secondary meaning as a person who "intended to mislead or cheat." The etymology of the word suggests that it derives from the Latin word "dehonestus" which means "unbecoming, improper, vulgar, or low-class."

Dishonesty is without a doubt a key component in the definition of any major form of acquisitive crime, and it serves as the center of gravity for the crimes listed in the Theft Act of 1968. The Act did not contain a definition of dishonesty, however, because of thehesitation on the part of Parliament.

Instead, Parliament approached the matter in a negative manner, by including a provision in Section 2(1) which states that three types of conduct are not to be regarded as dishonest.

This hint is supplemented by a single affirmative clause in Section 2(2), which states that a person may appropriate another's property dishonestly even if he is ready to pay for it. The main issue facing Parliament and the legal system is that it might be challenging to prove an act of dishonesty when it comes to a person's level of mental awareness.

Is it sufficient for a prosecutor to establish that a defendant is acting dishonestly where most people would consider that his conduct is dishonest but the defendant himself quite genuinely thought that he was not acting dishonestly, perhaps because he has a warped view of what is, and what is not, "untrustworthy, deceitful or insincere" conduct?

This kind of dishonesty is referred to as "objective dishonesty" because it occurs when someone is found to have violated the standards of other people's objective judgment. The alternate strategy is for the law to recognize dishonest behavior only in situations where the prosecution can demonstrate that the defendant was aware of and intended to engage in such behavior.

This type of dishonesty is called "subjective dishonesty" because it only considers a person's subjective mental state at the moment the wrongdoing was committed. A compromise definition of dishonesty that includes both objective and subjective components has been accepted by the English courts in an effort to give a useful definition against this backdrop.

2.3.2. Recklessness

The main issue with reckless risk-taking in the financial markets is whether reckless behavior can meet the standard of dishonesty for criminal law purposes. Similar to dishonesty, recklessness is a phrase that can be described in either objective or subjective terms as a reflection of a person's mental state.

Although there are some situations when the law approaches recklessness via an objective lens, it has been established law for the past 10 years that recklessness should be assessed using a subjective method when severe criminal action is involved.

The traditional definition of a conspiracy to defraud is the formation of an agreement between two or more defendants to falsely deny another person of something that is theirs, or to which they are, or would be, or may be entitled.

In Welham v. DPP, the House of Lords defined "fraud" as acting in a way that prejudges or taking the chance of prejudicing another's right while knowing that you have no legal justification for doing so. It is interesting to note that, even though "dishonestly" is routinely used instead of "fraudulently," Welham v. DPP makes no mention of the requirement for a judge to inform a jury that the accused was acting dishonestly.

As the learned editors of Archbold point out, the House of Lords must have considered it beyond argument that deliberately taking the risk of prejudicing another's right, knowing there is no right to do so, is necessarily dishonest. This line of reasoning is clearly illustrated by a consideration of the Court of Appeal rulings in the instances of R v. Sinclair and R v. Allsop. In R v. Sinclair, the defendants were found guilty of conspiring to defraud a corporation, its shareholders, and its creditors by utilizing the assets of the corporation for purposes other than those of the corporation.

According to the prosecution, the appellants, one of the company directors, and unidentified persons were all guilty of the crime because they had dishonestly agreed to take a risk with the business's assets in a way that was harmful to the interests of the minority shareholders.

The appellants claimed that this directive had the effect of inviting the jury to find them guilty of conspiring to defraud, regardless of whether they had a sincere notion that the victimized corporation would profit from their actions.

The Court of Appeal rejected this submission, making clear that "to cheat and defraud is to act with deliberate dishonesty to the prejudice of another person's proprietary right." The Court stated, the trial judge "had properly directed the jury as to the difference between the normal business risks taken honestly and the dishonest risk deliberately taken with knowledge that there was no right to take such risk."

Regarding reckless risk-taking on the financial markets, the denial of the appellant's claim that their conviction that the company's stockholders would ultimately profit from their reckless behavior had merit is evident.

A similar approach was taken by the Court of Appeal in R v Allsop when the Court affirmed the principle that a defendant could be guilty of participating in a conspiracy to defraud in circumstances where he did not intend that any actual loss would occur.

For a hire-purchase organization, the appellant served as a sub-broker who was tasked with introducing potential car buyers and handling their credit applications. In order to persuade the hire-purchase company to accept applications that they might have otherwise refused, the appellant occasionally provided misleading information on the application forms.

But the appellant always believed that the transactions would profit the hire-purchase company. In his appeal, the defendant claimed that the trial judge had erred by failing to instruct the jury that the prosecution required to show that the conspiracy's goal was to harm the hire buy corporation financially before a guilty conviction could be rendered.

Although it is true that irresponsible risk-taking on the financial markets does not always involve dishonest behavior, the statement of the principle that it suffices for the defendant's conduct to endanger the economic interests of another is important in this context.

Again, this is entirely consistent with the principle established in DPP v Welham that intentionally to take the risk of prejudicing another's right, knowing that there is no right to do so, is treated as necessarily dishonest.

Professor David Ormerod QC goes further and suggests that where conspirators know the effect of carrying out an agreement puts a person's property at risk, they are to be treated as if they intended to prejudice that person. If it later turns out that the individual's property is undamaged or even if the person who is at danger receives money from the deal, it makes no difference.

The idea that actual knowledge can be proven in criminal proceedings by a purposeful blindness to the possibility of negative outcomes is more widely applicable in other areas of criminal law.

For example, in Atwal v Massey, a case involving handling stolen goods where the establishment of guilty knowledge or belief for the purposes of Section 22 of the Theft Act 1968 (handling offense) was in issue, the High Court made clear that requisite mental element of the offense would be satisfied where it was shown that the defendant, "suspecting the goods to be stolen, deliberately shut his eyes to the consequences."

This strategy is completely in line with the formative analysis of criminal law knowledge presented a few years ago by Devlin J in Taylor's Central Garages (Exeter) Limited v. Roper.

Although these cases do not prove that dishonesty can be proven through evidence of careless risk-taking where a person closes their eyes to the risk, they are strongly in favor of this idea because they demonstrate that the necessary level of mental awareness for serious criminal offenses can be proven in this way.

2.3.3. Fraud by Abuse of Position

Section 4(1) of the Fraud Act 2006 provides that a person is guilty of fraud where he (i) occupies a position in which he is expected to safeguard, or not to act against, the financial interests of another person; (ii) he dishonestly abuses that position; and (iii) he intends, by means of the abuse of that position, to make a gain for himself or another, or to cause loss to another or to expose another to a risk of loss. The offense is punishable by a maximum of 10 years imprisonment.

Therefore, the act of making a high-risk investment on behalf of another person when it is unsuitable for their needs and the defendant is misusing his position to his personal advantage when doing so constitutes an offense.

The Law Commission had always anticipated that a defendant who acted in a way that endangered another person's economic interests would be guilty of fraud, and the elasticity of the offense to cover dishonest risk taking is not exceptional. The Law Commission's report on Fraud, which was released prior to the legislation's passage.

In his critique of the Fraud Act 2006, Professor David Ormerod QC notes that the potential range of defendants under Section 4 is vast since the term "abuse" is deliberately left undefined in order to maximize the breadth of the offense.

Furthermore, the misuse of the defendant's position is not confined to situations in which there is a fiduciary relationship between the defendant and the victim. Therefore, the necessary relationship will always exist anytime there is a link between a professional and his customer or between an employer and an employee.

Professor Ormerod concludes that Section 4 could be used in the prosecution of public officials for mismanagement of public funds since such individuals are expected to safeguard the financial interests of other people.

Since workers of financial institutions like investment banks are required to protect their employer's financial interests as well as the interests of the clients whose money, they are handling, there is seemingly no reason Section 4 should not be used in a prosecution of those employees.

2.3.4. A New Criminal Offence

Irrespective of whether or not Section 4 of the Fraud Act 2006 is sufficiently wide to capture the activities of reckless risk-taking on the financial markets, there are strong arguments for enacting a new criminal offense to this effect.

First, by establishing a crime involving careless risk-taking on the financial markets, participants in those markets, including traders and their managers, would receive a loud and clear message that decisions regarding the purchase and sale of investment securities, including derivatives, must be based on justifiable standards.

It would make it crystal apparent that speculative trading has no place on the financial markets, and it would enable rogue traders to face criminal charges for their fundamentally unlawful behavior in addition to those that are centered on their dishonest concealing of this behavior.

A new crime would also make top managers who themselves ignore a trader's speculative trading criminally accountable and subject to prosecution as either a major party due to his aiding and abetting, or as a secondary party for encouraging or providing help in the commission of a crime.

The new offense would also help protect the markets from unanticipated movements brought on by large amounts of speculative trading, in addition to protecting financial institutions like banks and their clients from the risk of suffering spectacular losses in situations where a trader has failed to gamble on market movements.

Second, establishing a crime for reckless risk-taking would be perfectly consistent with the fundamental ideas that guide the application of the criminal code.

The damage caused by the GFC is immense, and while it is impossible to determine how much careless risk-taking contributed to the economic disaster that struck the world in 2008, common sense suggests that it was unquestionably a factor.

The IMF has estimated the cost of the GFC at $11.9 trillion (£7.12 trillion) which is enough money to finance a £1,779 payment for every man, woman, and child on the planet. The IMF figures also show that the UK has been the biggest of all the spenders on emergency measures to support its financial sector, with its total bill for the clean-up amounting to 81.8% of its gross domestic product (GDP), equivalent to £1,227 billion.

The UK's record bill is also unique in that it has also already spent much of it already, with 20% of GDP having already supported struggling institutions.

The damage brought about by misbehavior on the financial markets in the UK is absolutely astounding. Given these facts, it is difficult to understand why the criminal law should continue to be powerless to hold financial market participants, including traders and senior management, accountable for facilitating reckless trading on the financial markets without carefully weighing the risks involved or, worse yet, without even a passing familiarity with those risks.

Powerful City traders and their managers would be held accountable in the same manner as others who engage in less serious financial misbehavior if there were a new criminal offense.

Thirdly, criminal law has long recognized recklessness as a legitimate yardstick for determining a person's level of guilt.

If it is a criminal act to recklessly damage physical property, recklessly make a misleading, false or deceptive promise or forecast to induce the making of a financial investment, or even recklessly transmit a sexual disease, there is no reason in principle or practice why there should not be a workable criminal offense of recklessly making decisions to buy or sell a financial instrument on the financial market.

2.3.5. Recklessly Managing a Bank

The UK Government has adopted a criminal offense that punishes the careless administration of a bank as one component of its response to the GFC. The new offense is contained in Section 36 of the Financial Services (Banking Reform) Act 2013 and provides that a senior manager of a financial institution commits a criminal offense punishable by a maximum period of seven years imprisonment if the following four elements can be proved:

- First, he must make a decision concerning the financial institution's business.
- Secondly, it must be demonstrated that when he makes the choice, he is aware of the possibility that doing so could result in the financial institution failing.
- Thirdly, the choice must significantly fall short of the standard that may be anticipated by someone in the senior manager's position.
- Fourthly, the implementation of the decision must cause the financial institution to fail.

According to a financial institution, a person is considered a senior manager if they carry out senior management duties. Section 19's definition of this job is that it involves managing one or more parts of the financial institution's affairs related to the activity that could have substantial repercussions for the manager or the financial institution's interests in the United Kingdom.

A financial institution is defined for the purpose of the criminal offense as a business which has permission under the Financial Services and Markets Act 2002 to continue the regulated activity of accepting deposits or is an investment firm within the meaning of Section 424A of that Act. When a financial institution becomes insolvent, Part 1 of the Banking Act of

2009 requires stabilization measures to be taken against it, or the Financial Services Compensation Scheme determines that it is unable or likely to be unable to pay any claims made against it, the financial institution will be deemed to have failed.

The offense is only committed when the manager senior recognized the risk and chose to disregard it by consciously closing his eyes to it, even if recklessness is not listed as a definitional part of the offense.

This reflects the legislative purpose signaled by the Parliamentary Commission on Banking Standards' finding that a strong case could be made for a new criminal offense of reckless behavior in bank management.

With the creation of a careless banking offense, the government has undoubtedly pioneered new territory. In an article in the Financial Times, a respected financial journalist noted that the creation of this offense has the potential to galvanize senior management, asking rhetorically how many British banks would have survived if cavalier senior managers had faced the risk of criminal prosecution for mismanagement on their watch?

However, the legislative initiative is restricted because the criminal offense is only committed when a senior manager does so, and the reckless risk-taking results in the downfall of a financial organization.

These prohibitions are pointless because, once the concept of criminal culpability for excessive risk-taking on the financial markets has been established, logic demands that it should apply to both market traders and senior managers.

Additionally, causing the financial institution the senior management and trader are employed by to go under should be dropped as a prerequisite need if the criminal offense is to have any real impact. There is no reason why it should be necessary in this circumstance, just as it is not necessary to prove the victim's complete destruction in cases of other financial market crimes.

If it is to respond more effectively to the challenges presented by the GFC, the UK Government needs to do more than dip its toe in the water as far as reckless risk-taking on the financial markets is concerned.

2.4. A NEW APPROACH TO FIGHT CRIME

In the 1970s and 1980s, the underground market for drugs multiplied by two, growing dramatically. Drug trafficking developed become a well-organized crime that frequently crossed international boundaries. In response, governments created legislation that aimed to stop both the drug trade itself and its support system on the financial front.

It is believed that targeting criminal profits can be a potent tool for justice, deterring people from committing crimes in the first place. Additionally, it provides police and prosecutors with tools to attack the criminal support system, which consists of individuals who aid the criminal organization but do not directly conduct the underlying crime (lawyers, accountants, and so on).

This is reflected in the United Nation's Vienna Convention (1988), which was the first global initiative to stem the tide of illicit profits from the narcotics trade. To further protect the financial system from being misused by drug trafficking groups, a task force was established by the G7 leaders in Paris in 1989 in accordance with the spirit of this Convention. The FATF was founded because of this.

The FATF quickly issued suggestions for the development of national mechanisms to identify and halt the flow of illegal money. Law enforcement would receive intelligence from the system to help them find criminals and those who assist them. The FATF suggested a number of particular actions that nations take to do this. The measures, which are extensive, are detailed in greater detail later in this chapter.

They demand that legislatures pass laws, that a number of public authorities be given more authority, that a portion of the private sector track the financial activities of its clients and report that information to the relevant authorities, that government agencies be given more authority to monitor compliance, and that these entities cooperate with one another and with other nations.

It takes a lot of organization, financial commitment, and, perhaps most significantly, political willingness to implement these recommendations in countries. There is no doubt that those who created the guidelines were aware of the difficulty, yet they still thought the rewards of following them would be worthwhile.

2.5. TOWARD STANDARD-SETTING

The FATF "recommendations" have evolved into the accepted guidelines for anti-money laundering (AML) over time. They have undergone two revisions, and a third is being worked on right now. With each modification, the range of illegal behaviors whose financial transactions are regarded as money laundering has significantly expanded. Now, other crimes like illegal logging and human trafficking are being prioritized rather than just drug revenues.

After the attacks on New York and Washington in 2001, the FATF added fighting the financing of terrorism to its goal, which was arguably the largest and most contentious expansion of the standards. The number of private organizations impacted by the criteria has therefore expanded. Now included in their scope are non-profit organizations, non-profit corporations, and non-profit professions.

It is crucial that each nation abide by the norms. First, it is essential that the standards be implemented globally because they are meant to address criminal activity that disregards national borders. Additionally, failing to comply might have serious repercussions for nations.

National AML/CFT regimes are assessed by the FATF, regional bodies, the World Bank, and the IMF. The assessments are known as "mutual evaluations" because representatives from the various bodies respect one another's conclusions. A number of name-and-shame measures may be taken against nations that are proven to be in violation of the law or uncooperative. For instance, in the year 2000, the Cook Islands were flagged as non-cooperative with the FATF standards.

The impact was severe, forcing the country to swiftly enact legislation and take other steps to improve its compliance with the FATF. As a result, foreign banks began closely examining any transactions involving the nation. To appreciate the level of impact, the enormous flight of foreign banks and offshore trusts reduced government revenue from the sector 70% in just the first three years of blacklisting.

Similarly negative effects were seen in Liechtenstein, where after two years on the blacklist, government revenue from the sector was cut in half. Numerous nations have been added to and removed from the FATF's blacklist since its founding in 1989, and the vast majority of them are developing nations. The 40 recommendations on money laundering and nine special recommendations on terrorist financing can be divided into five parts which are discussed in subsections.

2.5.1. Legal System

Ensuring that laws enable authorities the authority to pursue criminal cases and conduct investigations, take, and confiscate the victims' property, and collaborate with one another. Some sample questions that are asked in assessments of country compliance with this part of the standards include: How extensively does the law define money laundering? How dissuasive are the penalties for it?

2.5.2. Preventive Measures

Putting in place a regulatory regime that ensures key segments of the private sector are adequately identifying customers; keeping appropriate records; reporting suspicions to authorities; are supervised properly; have internal audit and compliance systems; and have measures to ensure legal entities (i.e., corporations, trusts, etc.) and are not fronts for criminal interests.

Some sample questions that are asked in assessments include: are banks required to keep customer records for at least five years? Are accountants obligated to report suspicious financial activity to the appropriate authority? Do financial institutions verify customers' identity appropriately?

2.5.3. Financial Intelligence Unit (FIU)

Establishing an intelligence agency that: collaborates with authorities both domestically and abroad to pursue investigations, analyzes data on suspected financial activity, generates leads for law enforcement, and assists prosecutors with evidence of unlawful cash transfers. Some sample questions that are asked in assessments include: Is the FIU independent? Does the FIU have the authority and resourcing to share intelligence information to other relevant authorities?

2.5.4. Mechanisms for Cross-Border Cooperation

Establishing procedures that permit domestic organizations to collaborate with one another across borders (prosecutors, police, etc.). Some sample questions that are asked in assessments include: Do authorities have an effective way to send and receive information from foreign jurisdictions? Does the country have an effective mechanism to respond to a foreign country's request to seize suspected laundered money?

2.5.5. Additional Elements for Combating the Financing of Terrorism (CFT)

These elements are meant to supplement and strengthen the AML controls previously discussed. Some sample questions that are asked in assessments include: Can authorities cooperate with foreign jurisdictions on terrorist financing related issues? Is terrorist financing a crime? Has the country ratified relevant UN conventions on terrorist financing?

2.6. THE INSTITUTIONS AND WHAT THEY DO

A large number of private organizations with experience in AML/CFT are expected to participate in the FATF regime. These private actors, which include financial institutions and "designated" non-financial firms and professions, should alert public authorities to any questionable consumer behavior, and create internal procedures to guard against being compromised by criminals.

In accordance with the FATF framework, public institutions compile the data in order to monitor, look into, and eventually prosecute. Additionally, they keep an eye on the private organizations to make sure that they have solid procedures in place to stop illegal activity using their services.

The many responsibilities that public institutions play in the AML/CFT regime are frequently comparable to those they perform in the larger financial regulatory framework. For instance, just as the Central Bank (or independent banking authority in some countries) is charged with supervising banks' prudential risk management practices, it frequently does the same for AML/CFT.

The scope and capabilities of public institutions may need to be expanded in countries implementing the FATF guidelines through legislation so that they can have jurisdiction to oversee AML/CFT issues. In this section we will outline the key roles each public institution holds in the typical FATF regime.

2.6.1. Policymakers

The main policy foundation for the AML/CFT regulatory system is established by the Ministry of Finance, the Treasury, or the Justice in the majority of countries. In some nations, this even entails presenting draft legislation to the parliament that would provide authorities a legal mandate and financial resources.

Others interpret it to suggest that it creates its own AML/CFT regulations. In still other cases, after the Central Bank creates regulations, it may simply approve them to ensure that they are consistent with policy.

The Policymaker is usually invariably the institution that decides the risk appetite for the AML/CFT regime, regardless of its specific responsibility, which is most significant. How strict do supervisors have to be with financial institutions? What ultimately determines how the regime thinks what risk-taking behaviors are acceptable and what are not is the overall tone set by the Policymaker.

The Central Bank or banking supervisor will highlight it in banking inspections and reprimand financial firms who employ it if the Policymaker feels a particular practice is too hazardous (i.e., it gives criminals too much opportunity to launder money).

2.6.2. Banking Supervisor

The Banking Supervisor transforms the high-level policies into particular rules and enforces them in the private sector, which is frequently the Central Bank or banking commission. It accomplishes this by establishing rules and instructions to financial institutions regarding their duties.

This same governmental entity frequently oversees the actual oversight, or supervision, of financial institutions' actions, thus it both creates the rules and controls how they are put into practice.

Most often AML/CFT supervision is included in a Banking Supervisor's work portfolio, however there are a significant number of exceptions to this supervisory model, which will be discussed later.

The Banking Supervisor typically conducts an inspection of financial institutions, scrutinizing paperwork, accounting records, and speaking with management and staff. A minor and frequently fresh portion of their concentration is AML/CFT.

It is significant to note that depending on the level of development of the country, the type of inspection might vary substantially. A one- to two-year interval is the norm for off-site assessments. There are fewer onsite audits.

2.6.3. Law Enforcement Agencies

The FATF refers to law enforcement agencies as encompassing a broad range of governmental institutions. The national police, customs agents, and border patrol are examples of organizations that are involved in law enforcement. The most important prerequisite for AML/CFT is that they have the resources and legal authority to look into potential AML/CFT issues.

Their involvement is crucial because they can connect the underlying crime to the proceeds of money laundering, or at the very least can offer information that does so. When it comes to fighting terrorism finance, investigators may already be looking into a suspected terrorist organization or individual. This could provide important knowledge.

For example, border patrol and customs officials are identified as key to prevent cross-border movements of illicit cash.

2.6.4. Judicial Authorities/Prosecutor

A case against an alleged criminal or group is sent to the legal system for prosecution if sufficient evidence has been obtained to support it. Legal authority is essential for prosecutors to pursue AML/CFT prosecutions. This invariably necessitates that these offenses be written into the law.

Prosecutors' involvement varies widely depending on the country, as do the time and approach. The FATF rules do not outline the proper procedure for bringing cases before a court, but they do state that sanctions must be proportionate and deterrent.

There should be open channels of communication between the police, supervisory agencies, prosecutors, and other pertinent parties. Although the prosecutor must sift through the information in these other public sources to get the evidence that would be admissible in court, the prosecutor's case heavily rests on the information obtained from them.

In the past, AML cases were frequently set aside so that prosecutors could focus on prosecuting offenders for the original crime rather than the money laundering that occurred later.

Enforcing compliance is a different potential role for judicial authorities. In order to accomplish this, they can assist the Central Bank or another AML/CFT supervisory body. When there is a case of flagrant violation of AML/CFT laws, the prosecutor is frequently summoned by banking supervisors in several countries.

The typical scenario is a financial institution that consistently fails to comply to the point where it borders on incompetence or even involvement with illicit activities. In a few rare instances, the Central Bank may refer the case for criminal court prosecution and sanctions.

2.6.5. Other Competent Authorities

Although the FATF standards' primary focus is financial institutions, they also cover a selection of "Designated Non-Financial Businesses and Professions" (DNFBPs). This group includes lawyers, dealers in precious stones, real estate agents and several others. Countries are given instructions to include certain groups in the AML/CFT regulatory framework according on the risk exposure of each organization in a particular jurisdiction.

To ensure that terrorist financing cannot be carried out through non-profit organizations, the FATF has made a special guideline for these institutions. Countries that determine a specific non-financial sector is vulnerable may develop new legislation or implement ones that already exist to include it in the AML/CFT framework.

This implies that additional regulatory agencies aside from those listed above may be engaged. For instance, it is usual for real estate brokers to be licensed and supervised by some sort of public entity, and casinos are frequently governed by a supervisory organization. These oversight bodies may enact AML/CFT regulations for a particular non-financial industry if they determine that it is susceptible to criminal misuse in some non-financial businesses or professions.

2.7. FINANCIAL INTELLIGENCE UNITS (FIUS)

It is expected that the FATF also requires that a body be established to store, assess, and disseminate data among agencies given the fact that its strategy for combating money laundering and terrorism funding is heavily data driven. To reduce the amount of fragmented data that has been collected is the goal.

To avoid being caught, criminals take advantage of the complexity of financial systems by dispersing their illegal activities among several institutions, industries, and regions. The FIU, which serves as the main repository of pertinent data, may fit these puzzle pieces together to aid law enforcement investigate a case and then support the judicial authorities in taking that case to court.

What kind of information do FIUs receive? FATF rules place a strong emphasis on the value of reports of suspicious transactions from financial institutions and other sources. The rules push nations to think about registering cash transactions so that the FIU is aware of any transactions that exceed a specific level.

Additionally, FIUs must have access to information used in law enforcement, administration, and finance. Specifically, this means information from the Central Bank or banking commission (e.g., bank licenses, banking supervision reports); police and border patrol (data from investigations, criminal records, customs declarations, border crossings); and other authorities (birth records, marriage certificates, company ownership).

With the help of all these data sources, FIUs have access to a significant amount of intelligence that they may examine and pass on to law enforcement in order to identify potential money launderers and terrorist financiers.

The FATF criteria are ambiguous on the formal investigative powers and organizational placement of a FIU within the government. Financial institutions may still alert law police to questionable customer behavior in nations where the FATF guidelines have not yet been completely implemented, either directly or via the Central Bank, which will then decide whether or not to alert law authorities.

Most countries do have a formal FIU; however, the type of FIU varies considerably. The following section outlines the three main types of FIUs though this is an arbitrary analysis and several countries have created FIUs that are fusions of all three types described here (Figure 2.2):

- Administrative model;
- Prosecutorial model; and
- Law enforcement model.

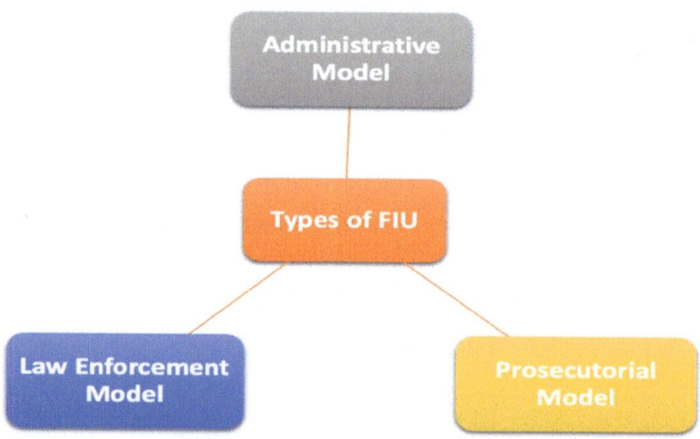

Figure 2.2. Types of FIU.

2.7.1. Administrative Model

The administrative model is the one that is used the most frequently by FIUs. The Central Bank, or occasionally the Ministry of Finance, houses administrative FIUs as an autonomous or semi-independent body. In accordance with this concept, FIUs serve as a bridge between law enforcement and financial institutions. An administrative FIU has this advantage, which is quite useful. Financial firms should feel more at ease disclosing sensitive information to the FIU because it is independent of the criminal justice system and a regulator.

They are aware that the FIU's authority is restricted to looking into financial crimes and does not extend as far as law enforcement or judicial authorities. Additionally, because this form of FIU has a single objective, there is no chance that AML/CFT will lose importance in favor of other criminal justice issues.

Due to their lack of authority to compel financial institutions to take action, administrative FIUs are occasionally seen as being weaker. It may be necessary to require a bank to quickly freeze any assets it holds that may be used to finance terrorism to prevent further investigation.

Administrative FIUs may also be viewed as weak depending on the nation because of their placement within the government's organizational structure. If a politician, such as the Minister of Finance, has the authority to monitor an administrative FIU, political influence may arise.

2.7.2. Prosecutorial Model

In countries with strict banking secrecy laws, administrative FIUs could have trouble. On the other hand, FIUs that are overseen by the prosecutor's office may be in a good position to obtain information from financial institutions where financial data is subject to a high level of legal protection. They also have the authority to search, detain, and interview individuals right away.

However, the fact that they have this authority can prevent them from developing a relationship with financial institutions where those institutions feel free to willingly give information. Without the assurance that their disclosure will not be used against them, banks, and other organizations are often reluctant to divulge information.

2.7.3. Law Enforcement Model

A law enforcement FIU is another FIU concept that is comparable to a prosecutorial one. Countries of this kind designate their FIUs as specialist divisions of the police force. Staff in such law enforcement models possess all or nearly all of the police's authority.

This entitles them to the right to search, question, and detain suspects. Law enforcement FIUs can obtain information that other models would not be able to. For instance, information sharing between national intelligence services and police is common, allowing law enforcement FIU to view information that other types may not.

However, this makes establishing solid information-sharing relationships with financial institutions difficult, much like with prosecutorial FIUs. Furthermore, they might not have the personnel to process the vast amounts of specialized financial, compliance, or other data that are necessary for identifying "dirty" financial institutions that collaborate with criminal interests.

If the police have a very inadequate financial skill set, they might not be well-equipped to detect money laundering through complicated financial items like stocks or derivative investments.

2.7.3.1. Relations Management with the FATF

The FIU is the center for AML/CFT intelligence and domestic and international information sharing but it is never the representative to the FATF or FATF-styled regional body. Discussions in the FATF are about high-level policies so FIUs do not typically attend FATF meetings.

The major representative of the nation in the FATF is typically the body responsible for domestic policy, such as the Ministry of Finance or Treasury. Because of this, it is crucial that the representative is knowledgeable about the problems that exist, how the regulated industries operate, and the criminal landscape in their nation. Internationally agreed-upon high standards are beneficial when they draw on the experience of actually putting them into effect.

2.8. COMMON CHALLENGES IN DEVELOPING COUNTRIES

It is difficult for all nations to become fully compliant with the FATF framework because it is meant to be comprehensive. In actuality, no nation has ever been judged to be totally in compliance with all FATF recommendations, and certain recommendations have never been judged to be fully in compliance in any nation.

The complex, costly, and highly required legal, institutional, and diplomatic actions that countries must take involve all levels of public institutions. Both wealthy and poor nations struggle to achieve all FATF compliance requirements.

Additionally, with a few significant exceptions, there is a consistent tendency that links economic progress with FATF compliance levels positively. Truthfully, developed nations typically perform worse on examinations than wealthy nations.

The methodology and capacity of execution in these nations are the root causes of this tendency. It could also be attributed to the institutional approach that the standards themselves recommended to reduce money laundering and terrorist financing.

2.8.1. Institutional Capacity

Without a doubt, a nation's institutional capacity and its adherence to the FATF standards are closely related. Staff training, numbers, and budgetary resources are critical to build the well-functioning AML/CFT regime envisioned by the standards.

Governments in developing nations frequently lack the budgetary resources needed to establish the numerous specialized public institutions found in rich nations. Additionally, even when such entities as a FIU do exist, they are frequently underfunded, understaffed, or lacking in training.

What happens when an agency has insufficient budgetary capacity or staff training to play its role in the AML/CFT regime? This often results in what one African FIU chief jokingly called, "suffocation by paper." Piles of documents build up:

There is a lot to evaluate, including Central Bank data, suspicious transaction reports from financial institutions, customs declarations, police records, and so forth. Investigations will proceed slowly and ineffectively if there are not enough trained employees.

According to empirical data, a nation's compliance with the FATF affects how large its financial sector is within its economy. Even in regions with a tiny financial industry, which is sometimes thought to make it "easier" for public authorities to regulate, this is frequently the case.

Contrary to popular belief, a new review of 161 nation assessment reports by the IMF20 shows that there is a direct correlation between a country's adherence to the FATF and the size of its financial sector. Countries with large financial sectors (in terms of employment, market size, and other factors) are more compliant than countries with tiny financial sectors.

This would lend credence to the idea that finding sufficient technical talent in the latter set of nations is difficult. Even if a nation has the financial resources to establish the public institutions envisioned by the standards, this does not ensure that there are sufficient technical specialists available to ensure effectiveness.

In low-capacity countries, a banking supervisor's or FIU analyst's day sometimes involves dealing with an overwhelming amount of data, likely because of financial or technical constraints. As a result, many chores become daunting and highly ineffective. In more developed nations, FIUs train analysts and typically manage electronic documents and computer access.

Technology and adequate expertise enable fast data searches that deliver pertinent answers to requests from the legal or judicial systems in a timely manner. Investigations can go more quickly because of the quick information delivery.

It enables law enforcement personnel to have the resources they require to obtain subpoenas, detain offenders, and bring a case to a successful conclusion. The other governmental institutions in poor nations frequently receive minimal support from FIUs because they are so frequently delayed, forcing them to rely on their own information silos to function.

The FATF methodology heavily relies on statistics. The FIU should be able to effectively store and analyze enormous amounts of different data. Being assessed as non-compliant with the pertinent FATF requirements is a result of developing nation FIUs frequently lacking this money and staff technical capacity. In addition, it goes beyond merely being a capacity concern for FIU.

Many developing nations lack adequate border or police force training. Most of the time, judges, and prosecutors lack the expertise or experience necessary to manage the complexities of a money laundering or terrorism funding case. These are all challenges that are frequently brought up in developing nations. FATF evaluations.

2.8.2. Prioritization

A low degree of priority for AML/CFT might undermine the regime's ability to function, even in locations where capacity and coordination are not problems. Most of the time, the causes of this are clear. They view policy concerns as being significantly more essential than AML/CFT, particularly in developing nations that are among the poorest or most prone to war. Examples of this abound anecdotally. The head of one Middle Eastern country's intelligence agency said "Terrorist financing means nothing to us;

terrorists are coming across the border and bringing bombs with them. Our money is better spent buying bomb-sniffing dogs than hiring FIU analysts.

Money laundering and terrorism financing may simply be ignored in other poor nations. They believe that the FATF's goals are driven by industrialized nations' worries about white-collar financial crimes, which do not exist in their nation.

Alternately, they can acknowledge that such crimes do occur within their jurisdiction but that they are not as serious as other development requirements like constructing schools, immunizing kids, or offering fundamental, on-the-street police services.

2.9. RECKLESS AUTOMATION IN POLICING

A growing amount of policing decisions are being made automatically. Robotics, facial recognition, predictive analytics, and license plate readers have all been used to supplement conventional police investigation techniques. With the use of these tools, the police are able to sort through vast amounts of data at a scale and pace that are not possible using only human skills.

However, this dependence on AI has raised a lot of issues on how to strike a balance between the necessity for criminal investigations and worries about fairness, bias, openness, and accountability. These issues are not particular to the police. You can find similar calls for "algorithmic accountability" in healthcare, banking, credit scoring, public benefits, and employment.

2.10. AUTOMATION AND ACCOUNTABILITY

We all know about the influence of artificial intelligence and automation in our lives, from the most mundane experiences, like picking favorite songs or movies, to more important decisions like who should receive job interviews or who should receive government benefits.

Police work also includes that automation. License plate readers use algorithms today to swiftly recognize certain plates. In real-time scans or fixed databases, facial recognition technology can quickly recognize faces. High-risk people and locations are identified by software. The term "artificial intelligence" refers to the use of machines to perform cognitive tasks that are typically completed by people. All of this automation falls under this category. That is an inclusive concept, and for good reason: artificial intelligence can encompass anything from the use of simple algorithms to more intricate examples of machine learning that adapt to find patterns in data (Figure 2.3).

Figure 2.3. Facial recognition technology.

Source: Image by Wikimedia Commons.

Risk assessments in finance are an example of artificial intelligence that only gives decision-makers more information, whereas other types actually carry out the analysis and take the appropriate action (hiring and employment decision making).

But automation also poses questions about bias, secrecy, unaccountability, and mistakes that are hard to spot when the decision originates from a machine and not a person. While the United States lacks a comprehensive data protection regime, many regulatory approaches have been proposed and some have become law.

These recommendations can be made with regard to automated decision-making generally or with regard to more niche topics like law enforcement and criminal justice.

In a similar vein, the algorithms themselves may be biased. Algorithms are created by people, and their presumptions on the proper structuring and application of the algorithm may lead to further biases.

A recruitment algorithm, for instance, which uses men as the model for professional "fit" will disadvantage female applicants. Bias is, of course, not a novel concept. However, bias can amplify disparities in this situation by duplicating these effects on a large scale, whether it is in the training data or the instructions themselves. Public access to data sets and source codes has been suggested as a resolution by some academics.

The call for explain ability is another suggestion made in artificial intelligence policy. Some sophisticated applications of artificial intelligence may be so complex that programmers are unable to precisely explain why or how certain results were attained.

This black box problem means that a person may not be able to know why a particular prediction or decision was made. Thus, there have been calls for a "right to explanation" when, for example, a person receives an adverse employment decision through automation.

And although calling for the explanation of why an automated process led to a person's rejection for a loan, a job, or benefits has appeal, there is not yet widespread consensus on what form that explain ability should take. To give people "technology due process" rights in automated decision-making, the right to an explanation can be used in conjunction with other instruments from a legal framework.

2.11. AUTOMATION, BIOETHICS, AND POLICING

How can such a vastly different conversation on law and policy regarding human subject research inform the one in police automation? There are numerous solutions to the issues with automation put forth by the algorithmic accountability movement. However, these discussions initially center on technology: how to alter, reform, and keep track of both the data and the layout of automated decision making.

All of this remains important. But to pose the question as the beginning of this topic of the chapter: what if we think of new forms of automated decision making in policing as experiments on communities that might impose harm with life altering decisions?

First, we are aware that diverse types of surveillance are used unevenly throughout society. Receiving public benefits frequently entails submitting to privacy-invading inquiries, fingerprinting, drug testing, and verification requirements. Contrary to their wealthier and whiter counterparts, non-white, low-income areas are more frequently subject to draconian police presence and surveillance.

Due to their tendency to purchase less expensive digital equipment with fewer privacy protections and their lack of digital literacy, low-income

Americans suffer disadvantages online. Low-wage work is particularly subject to tracking movements, productivity, drug tests, and other forms of surveillance.

Furthermore, low-income, non-white communities experience more monitoring overall than other groups do, as well as more surveillance in combination. Living under constant and inescapable observation has very real potential negative effects.

It can be challenging for residents of low-income neighborhoods to maintain their privacy and to correct errors that result in unfavorable choices about housing, credit, and law enforcement. This indicates that some communities have less freedom and privacy from observation than other groups.

In the case of policing, we might consider the decision to "test" out a new automated decision-making on a community as a form of experimentation with impacts that might benefit from the ethical concerns in human subjects' research.

Currently, when a law enforcement agency chooses to pilot or implement automated decision-making, it may do so without consulting, soliciting input from, or informing the community it polices. It may also do so without explicitly evaluating whether the experiment maximizes benefits while minimizing harms, or it may do so without evaluating whether a program burdens the community in question.

Without receiving ethical clearance, we would not support a medical test on a group of people that might have psychological and physical effects. But new police technologies typically do not consider any of the ethical norms that are basic to research with human people.

When we know that police agencies do in fact experiment with and occasionally abandon computerized decision-making programs that have greatly impacted the affected communities, the lack of such ethical considerations is startling. Consider this recent example.

To identify those who were most likely to become victims or perpetrators of gun violence over the course of the following 18 months, the Chicago Police Department started using risk models in 2012. These models are known as their "Heat Lists."

The risk models were developed by a research team from the Illinois Institute of Technology, and the "scores" for people—everyone who had been arrested in the preceding four years—were determined based on those models. The risk score determines how likely it is that a person will become "Party to Violence," either as a victim or an offender of gun violence (Figure 2.4).

Figure 2.4. Illinois Institute of Technology.

Source: Image by Flickr.

These scores were available to all Chicago Police Department personnel, as well as on its crime mapping software. By 2018, there were nearly 4,00,000 people with individualized risk scores under the program. The majority of black men in Chicago between the ages of 20 and 29 had a risk score under the program.

It its 2020 report, the City of Chicago's Inspector General found the department's predictive program filled with "concern[s]." The individualized scores and risk tiers used in the program were found to be "unreliable."

Furthermore, the scores—which were based on arrests that might not have resulted in convictions—could have served as the impetus for police interventions that "essentially punished persons for criminal conduct for which they had not been convicted."

Even though they were never found guilty of the earlier arrest, some people may have faced tougher charging judgments in later arrests if they had a high-risk score. The Department formally decommissioned the program in November 2019.

The risk assessment program used in Chicago is an example of reckless automation. Armed with a new data-driven project and $3.8 million dollars in federal funding, the police department experimented with a program that led to numerous "Custom Notification Program" interventions: visits to the homes of persons identified as high risk.

These encounters were technically described as chances to introduce high-risk individuals to social service initiatives, but in many instances, they may have amounted to little more than "going door to door warning potential criminals not to commit any violent crimes."

2.12. CONCLUSION

This chapter provides an overview of the financial markets' risk, heedlessness, and regulation. Securitization, irrational risk-taking, and the world financial crisis were covered at the beginning of this chapter. A new strategy for combating crime, standard settings, and carelessness are some other themes covered in this chapter.

This chapter includes highlights on the administrative, prosecutorial, and law enforcement models of FIUs in its middle section. The common difficulties faced by developing nations and the careless automation of law enforcement are also explained in this chapter. By the chapter's conclusion, topics like policing, bioethics, and automation & accountability had been covered.

REFERENCES

1. *Financial Intelligence Units,* (2022). Egmont Group. Available at: https://egmontgroup.org/about/financial-intelligence-units/ (accessed on 15 June 2023).
2. Hollywood, J. S., (2016). *CPD's 'Heat List' and the Dilemma of Predictive Policing*. RAND Corporation. Available at: https://www.rand.org/blog/2016/09/cpds-heat-list-and-the-dilemma-of-predictive-policing.html (accessed on 15 June 2023).
3. *Policing Financial Services – GSMA,* (n.d.). gsma.com. Available at: https://www.gsma.com/mobilefordevelopment/wp-content/uploads/2012/06/policingfinancialservicessurveyingtheantimoneylaunderingregulatoryregime2011.pdf (accessed on 15 June 2023).
4. *Reckless Automation in Policing* – btlj.org (n.d.). Available at: https://btlj.org/wp-content/uploads/2022/07/BTLJ-Joh_WebVersion_07-10-22.pdf (accessed on 15 June 2023).
5. *Risk Recklessness and Policing the Financial Markets,* (n.d.). Available at: https://www.devereuxchambers.co.uk/assets/docs/publications/risk_recklessness_and_policing_the_financial_markets_jf_2015.pdf (accessed on 15 June 2023).
6. Smyth, E., (2014). *New Offence of "Reckless Management of a Bank" – Will it be Effective? and What Are the Risks?* Lexology. Kingsley Napley. Available at: https://www.lexology.com/library/detail.aspx?g=fc5380c8-f4f9-456b-bc3e-e997eab65774 (accessed on 15 June 2023).

CHAPTER 3

Credible Deterrence and Consumer Protection Through the Imposition of Financial Penalties

Contents

This chapter talks about credible deterrence and consumer protection through the imposition of financial penalties. At the beginning of this chapter, this chapter explains about the understanding deterrence, definitions, and its types. The chapter also addresses the three fundamental conditions for successful deterrence and some concerns with credible deterrence in theory and practice. The chapter also highlights the types of firms and proportionality and consequentialist focus.

3.1. UNDERSTANDING DETERRENCE

The difficulty of deterrence – preventing states from acting unintentionally, especially through military aggression – has once more emerged as a central concern in American defense policy. In Europe, the United States and its allies seek to deter potential Russian adventurism in the Baltic states, as well as "gray-zone" activities (ongoing belligerence below the threshold of major war).

Along with preventing an actual invasion, the United States and the Republic of Korea cooperate to thwart various provocations by North Korea in Korea. China's aggressiveness and gray-zone incursions into regions where there are territorial disputes are issues that the United States and its allies are dealing with elsewhere in Asia.

Since the end of the Cold War, the United States has never faced a more urgent need for effective deterrence than it does today, across the globe and in many other fields. Furthermore, the risks of actually waging a large war are greater than ever, making it even more crucial to prevent conflict, as many possible opponents are substantially more capable than they were 10 or more years ago.

However, a lot of the current deterrence discussion still relies heavily on assertions without evidence, claims that are at odds with the available data, and little citations of earlier studies. The setting for deterrence has changed because of changes in the global security environment, potentially contradicting long-held beliefs and generating new demands.

This perspective revisits core ideas and principles concerning deterrence by drawing on a variety of contemporary and vintage Corporation research. The main takeaway from this study is that deterrence and dissuasion must be viewed as an effort to change a potential aggressor's perspective.

Deterrent policies are often viewed through the perspective of the country doing the deterring—in this case, the United States – and focus on actions that it takes to raise the costs and risks of an attack. But the value of those steps depends entirely on their effect on the perceptions of the target state.

Any strategy to prevent aggression must begin with an assessment of the interests, motives, and imperatives of the potential aggressor, including its theory of deterrence (taking into account what it values and why).

In the process, as will be argued, history strongly suggests that aggressor motivations are varied and complex, and as often grounded in a desperate sense of a need to function as they are the product of aggressive opportunism.

Deterrence turns out to include considerably more than just posing a danger to a potential foe: It necessitates the subtle manipulation of perceptions so that a potential enemy views peaceful alternative to attack as more desirable than conflict.

3.2. DEFINITIONS AND TYPES

Deterrence is the process of preventing someone—in international politics, typically a nation-state—from pursuing undesirable acts, like launching an armed attack. Contrary to the similar but separate idea of "corpulence," which includes trying to persuade an actor to do something, it entails an effort to stop or avoid an action (Figure 3.1).

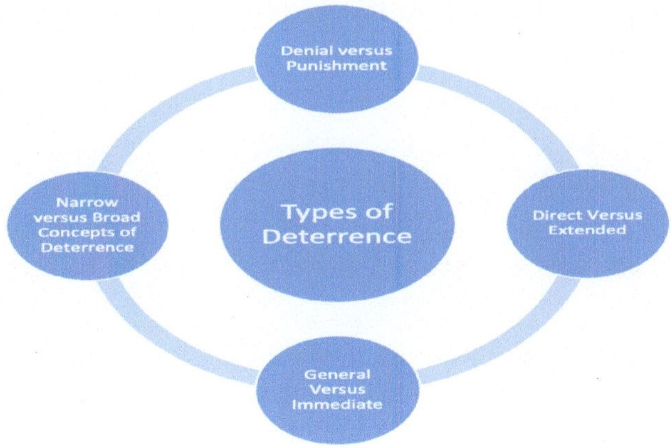

Figure 3.1. Types of deterrence.

3.2.1. DENIAL VERSUS PUNISHMENT

There are two primary methods of deterrence that are distinguished in classic literature. Through making a potential aggressor's actions impossible or unlikely to succeed, deterrence by denial tactics try to undermine their confidence in achieving their goals. For instance, they might mobilize enough local military forces to repel an invasion.

These tactics have the potential to expose a potential aggressor to the possibility of irreparable harm. Deterrence through denial is nothing more than the application of a desire and an effort to uphold a commitment.

The power to defend is equivalent to the ability to deny; "deterrence and defense are conceptually distinct but integrally connected in practice." The immediate balance of forces in the contested region is the most popular metric for assessing the strength of a deterrence threat based on denial capabilities; but, as demonstrated, the local balance of forces is not the only or even always the most significant aspect.

It is incorrect to only think of military balances when discussing deterrence by denial. On the other side, deterrence via punishment foresees harsh costs, such as nuclear escalation or severe economic sanctions, should an assault take place. The local conflict and the global community are tied by these sanctions.

Threats of harsher punishment, which would make an attack more expensive, are the main component of punishment-based deterrence, not the direct defense of the contested commitment. Denial methods are often seen as being more dependable than punishment strategies, according to the majority of classic studies. Actions taken to deny, such as placing large military capabilities squarely in an aggressor's path, speak out strongly.

However, a defender's desire to exact sanctions might be questioned by an aggressor. Additionally, an aggressor may persuade itself that the defense would hold off on enforcing punishment threats due to the dangers that come with them, such as the potential for further escalation and the possibility that the state acting as a deterrent may not be willing to flee when the time comes.

As Thomas Schelling noted, there are threats that a state would rather not fulfill, and weakness in deterrence can emerge when an aggressor believes the defender will ultimately prove unwilling to carry out its threats.

3.2.2. Direct versus Extended

There are two situations in which deterrence can be applied. In order to avoid attacks on its own territory – in the instance of the United States, within its own borders—a state must use direct deterrence. Extended deterrence involves preventing assaults on third parties, such as partners or allies.

During the Cold War, direct deterrence involved discouraging a Soviet nuclear attack on U.S., territory; extended deterrence involved preventing a Soviet conventional attack on North Atlantic Treaty Organization (NATO) members.

Extended deterrence presents greater challenges than direct deterrence for obvious reasons. This is partially accurate due to military operational needs: An attack that requires the deployment of military power, often thousands of miles distant and frequently considerably closer to the territory of the aggressor state, is harder to refute than one that occurs close to home. However, it is also true for reasons of credibility.

A state's ability to defend itself against aggressors can always be relied upon, while a defender's ability to stand up for a third party may be in dispute. The American pledge to "sacrifice New York for Paris," for instance, was the subject of ongoing discussion throughout the Cold War.

Taking action to persuade an aggressor that the distant defender would unquestionably defend itself against an assault, or at the very least will do so as quickly as it can in compliance with national rules, is a key component of enhancing extended deterrence.

Such measures include placing a sizable contingent of troops from the state that is acting as a deterrent on the territory of the country that is under threat, as the United States has frequently done. When an ally is attacked, the defense tries to give the impression that it has no other alternative but to take action.

However, this is a difficult condition to fulfil, in part because a state rarely agrees to something resembling an automatic reaction if crucial national interests are not at risk – and frequently even if they are.

The most famous cases of extended deterrence failure involving the United States - such as Korea in 1950 and Iraq-Kuwait in 1990— can be partly traced to the fact that the United States was unwilling to demonstrate automaticity of response before the fact. Even the most powerful treaty commitments generally contain some degree of leeway.

3.2.3. General versus Immediate

The theoretical literature also distinguishes between two overlapping temporal windows for the application of deterrence measures. The long-term, consistent effort to stop undesirable behaviors in circumstances other than emergencies is known as general deterrence. In times of crisis, immediate deterrence refers to more immediate, urgent efforts to stop a specific, impending attack.

For example, the United States employed general deterrence for decades by publicizing ongoing promises of defense and punishment if the Soviet Union attacked Western Europe. When a crisis arose and the US believed Soviet assault against Berlin was about to begin, the country engaged in the related but different duty of urgent deterrence.

According to the majority of traditional studies, general deterrence is simpler than immediate deterrence. Long stretches of time may go by before an aggressor is tempted to behave aggressively. Deterrence is most vulnerable when violence seems highly appealing or urgently necessary, and these circumstances demand extremely forceful and urgent actions to support immediate deterrence.

Success in these situations can be particularly difficult since the aggressor may have developed a strong commitment to a course of action and a strong aversion to giving up, making it impossible to dissuade them.

As a result, one of the objectives of general deterrence is to lessen the need for rapid deterrence by fostering deterrent and dissuasion effects that become so engrained that refraining from attacking becomes routine.

3.2.4. Narrow versus Broad Concepts of Deterrence

One of the most important decisions about how to view deterrence involves its scope: Is it viewed narrowly or broadly? The most restrictive definitions stipulate that deterrence only applies to military instruments of statecraft, employing the threat of a military reaction to stop a state from acting.

A larger definition of deterrence maintains the emphasis on threats but broadens the range of responses to non-military ones: a state can use the threat of economic penalties, diplomatic exclusion, or information operations to deter. The basic definition of deterrence is "dissuasion by way of threat," which is supported by both strategies.

It can be based on "the capability of defense denying the adversary its immediate objectives" or on "the threat of inflicting heavy punishment in a larger struggle." In either case, there is an attempt to change how risk and cost are calculated by endangering the aggressor's other interests or future success. A third, more comprehensive method of viewing deterrence is to consider deterrence as one step in a bigger process of convincing a potential actor to refrain from engaging in undesirable behavior that includes means other than threats.

Dissuasion aims to persuade a potential aggressor that the cost-benefit analysis of aggressiveness is unfavorable, in part by highlighting the costs of aggression but also by providing reassurances and rewards that make a world without hostility more alluring. It's a strategy meant to make violence both useless and expensive.

"In its most general form," Alexander George and Richard Smoke have written, "deterrence is simply the persuasion of one's opponent that the costs and/or risks of a given course of action he might take outweigh its benefits."

According to this idea, deterrent tactics can help avoid an action by taking measures to render it unnecessary, such as by making concessions or assuring people not to take the action in the first place.

3.3. THREE FUNDAMENTAL CONDITIONS FOR SUCCESSFUL DETERRENCE

Numerous deterrence studies have identified three key elements as the most crucial determinants of the success or failure of deterrence strategies. These studies range from wholly theoretical to game theory-based to large-scale statistical analyzes of deterrence cases and detailed case studies of specific examples.

3.3.1. Level of Aggressor Motivation

The potential aggressor's intentions are the starting point for any examination of deterrence success or failure, as evidenced by the significance of perceptual factors to deterrence. A state will not be difficult to dissuade from engaging in aggression if it finds little justification for doing so, but it may become impossible to stop if it has grown to believe that only an attack will protect its interests.

Patrick Morgan concludes that "challenger motivation is the most important factor in deterrence success or failure." Many impressions, not all of which are opportunistic, may serve as justification for an assault. In fact, one of the strongest motivators of aggressive intent is how much a potential aggressor disapproves of the current situation.

A state that believes that it is being constricted to the point of regime collapse, such as Iraq in 1990 or Japan in 1941, will accept many more risks than a state that believes it can achieve its national goals without war. The empirical record strongly suggests that states that launch aggressiveness are not only opportunistic or aggressive but are frequently responding to conditions they regard as particularly hazardous.

Combinations of threats and concessions appear to be most associated with deterrence success; as one scholar has concluded, "Mixing deterrence and conciliation is best—be tough but not bullying, rigid, or unsympathetic." These decisions are typically comparative rather than binary.

Rarely do decision-makers analyze the relative merits of a number of alternative pathways while weighing the cost-benefit analysis of beginning violence. If leaders believe that attacking is less expensive or risky than any of the alternatives, they won't be discouraged.

However, this process of comparing alternatives also implies, as Schelling contended, that "the pain and suffering" represented by the deterrent threats "had to appear depending on their action." Deterrent threats may lose their effectiveness as a tool for stopping actions if they become to be viewed as part of a wider antagonism strategy.

3.3.2. Clarity About the Object of Deterrence and Actions the Defender Will Take

A second broad criterion for deterrence success is that the defender should be as clear as possible about what it is trying to deter, as well as what it will do if the threat is ignored. Korea in 1950 and Iraq in 1990 provide two powerful examples of the dangers of a striking absence of clarity. In both cases, the United States refused to be clear in its deterrent threat.

Due to this failure, two aggressive individuals with elevated levels of motivation had plenty of time to persuade themselves that they could accomplish their goals without prompting a strong American response. By its nature, deterrence is a demand that another state refrains from doing something.

There is a greater probability that the deterrence policy will fail the vaguer the demand. The deterring state's pledges must be specific, and their target must be able to comprehend them. Getting the word across "through the din and cacophony" of global politics to a potential attacker is a crucial problem for deterrent threats.

To convey a clear message, this necessitates both public and private initiatives. It also emphasizes the peril of making claims or taking acts that appear to cast doubt on the sincerity of the commitment. However, as was previously stated , issuing unwarranted deterrent threats can be expensive, both in terms of the military requirements they create and because of the hatred and tensions they incite—tensions that could wind up making a confrontation more likely rather than less likely.

States attempting to thwart an attack must constantly strike a balance between these critical factors, attempting to achieve a level of transparency that will reveal their goals without triggering. And in the process, the defender is always calculating the degree of national interests involved:

Even if it would prefer to prevent a certain type of aggression, it will rarely be able to broadcast clear deterrent threats during times of peace if the target of the assault is not crucial to the state acting as a deterrent.

3.3.3. Aggressor Must Be Confident That Deterring State Has Capability and Will to Carry Out Threats

Much of classic deterrence theory can be boiled down to a simple proposition: The potential aggressor must have faith in the defender's competence and motivation to conduct its threats.

This criterion is, again, perceptual – the question is not whether the defender actually has such capabilities or will, it is whether the aggressor believes that it does. Deterrence depends on the perception of the "threatener's determination to fulfill the threat if need be"—and, more importantly, on the potential aggressor's "conviction that the threat will be carried out."

When an attacker determines that the defender's threat is unlikely to be conducted, deterrence fails, according to Bruce Russett. In this idea, the two distinctive components of capability and will are highlighted. If either is thought to be weak, deterrence may be compromised. The concept of capability is straightforward.

As previously mentioned, the immediate, local balance of forces is not always a key factor in determining the effectiveness of deterrence; however, a defender's broadly perceived suite of capabilities, military, and non-military, must be strong enough to persuade a potential attacker that it will pay a high price for aggression. Much more ethereal and open to misunderstanding is the variable of will. Particularly in situations of prolonged deterrence, attackers have frequently persuaded themselves that a defense lacked the resolve to protect oneself. Will is partially influenced by the national interests at stake: If a potential attacker perceives that a defense has important interests at risk, they are more likely to believe threats of retaliation.

To change the facts on the ground without ever engaging in behavior that would justify a significant response, aggressors may use "salami slicing" strategies to try to undercut a defender's willingness to retaliate.

Such strategies are designed to put the defender in a dilemma: It cannot respond to every small violation, but if it does not begin to punish minor transgressions, its strategic position will erode over time. The United States confronts this challenge with Chinese and Russian gray-zone campaigns today.

As was previously stated, the traditional theory of deterrence stressed the importance of both issuing credible threats and, whenever possible, generating a sense of obligation to act. Schelling argued that if a war were imminent, the deterring state would frequently try to escape the obligations of such agreements by reneging on its deterrent threats.

Some aggressors may anticipate this and believe themselves that threats will be abandoned once the dangers become excessive, leading to deterrence failing even in the presence of rhetorical pledges.

Sustaining a potential aggressor's belief in the threats became a major preoccupation of the deterrence literature, and Schelling brought the line of thinking to its natural conclusion: To deter, stating a commitment is not enough; a defender must show that it has no choice but to react.

The literature offers a number of specific methods for forging such irrevocable pacts, including making unambiguous public commitments and staking national prestige on a strong response; signing formal treaties of mutual defense; deploying trip wire forces; building a basing and logistical infrastructure that signals an intention to bolster in the event of war; and selling weapons to the threatened state to strengthen defense ties.

However, as was previously mentioned, making vows that cannot be broken comes with extremely high political costs and is frequently more than a defense is ready to do in a period of peace. Finally, the notion that a state's overall reputation for toughness and resolution is crucial to deterrence has now been largely disproven. This argument regarding the credibility of deterrent threats has long been maintained.

This claim supported the idea, which guided much of U.S. Cold War policy, that no example of Soviet aggression could be ignored. Because reputation was thought to accumulate through individual actions, standing firm across the board seemed essential. In particular situations, reputations – national or personal – can be important. States and leaders occasionally make decisions based in part on stereotype-like perceptions of national resolve, and individual leaders do work to build their reputations within the international system.

The notion that a country's reputation is a single, unified good, similar to a bank account, whose overall value influences potential aggressors' calculations and is a key factor in deciding deterrence outcomes, has been largely refuted by contemporary studies.

Multiple studies have demonstrated that leaders make situational, rather than dispositional, judgments about resolve—they ask whether a defender would fulfill a commitment in a specific case or context, rather than inferring general rules from a defender's overall track record.

Reputational obligations are not interdependent: An adversary's belief that a state would respond on other issues may not be affected by a state's failure to respond in one instance.

This conclusion has been changed by several studies arguing that encounters with a possible foe within a recent time frame may have an impact on risk assessment and, consequently, the likelihood of aggression. Therefore, reaching a compromise with one particular potential attacker might make it more likely for it to subsequently raise a deterrence-related objection.

3.4. SOME CONCERNS WITH CREDIBLE DETERRENCE IN THEORY AND PRACTICE

The FCA's enforcement approach is built around credible deterrence. Regulators may have a legitimate desire to present themselves as fearless enforcers, which is certainly understandable. Particularly in the case of organizations that have come under fire for alleged inadequate enforcement and oversight. The FSA, for example, was avowedly 'light touch' but was claimed by some critics to be 'soft touch.' It is understandable that a financial regulator would want to establish its authority given the ongoing global financial crisis (GFC) and the general concern over financial misbehavior.

It is also clear that the Regulator accepts the essential premise of deterrence outlined above. In the words of Tracey McDermott 'To achieve credible deterrence, wrongdoers must not only realize that they face a real and tangible risk of being held to account but must also expect to face a meaningful sanction.' This emphasis on credible deterrence, however, creates a number of serious issues.

3.5. TYPES OF FIRMS AND (DIS)PROPORTIONALITY

Although theories of optimal deterrence are essentially predicated on the idea that businesses are impersonal cost-benefit calculators, many businesses will not implement the type of cost-benefit analysis that is envisioned. In addition to avoiding penalties, businesses follow the law for a variety of additional reasons. These motivations include a sense of obligation and custom, as well as reverence for the rule of law.

Ayres and Braithwaite have commented that many firms will comply with the law most of the time 'because it is the law.' Many authorities are reluctant to regularly pursue enforcement action because they believe that most businesses are motivated to comply and that most violations are unintentional.

The above-mentioned optimal deterrence approach is therefore only partially useful in cases when a corporation is not specifically inclined to break the law. It is potentially challenging to prevent negligence because, in practice, many violations happen when businesses act carelessly rather than consciously.

Instead of deliberate misbehavior, a lot of FSMA violations happen when businesses have insufficient controls, supervision, and structure.

There are concerns regarding whether an emphasis on deterrence is appropriate when breaches happen accidentally rather than due to something more nefarious. First, a focus on deterrence in such situations is useless (and even destructive), and second, it is unfair. These are the two main criticisms (which may, in turn, lead to it being even less effective).

Effectiveness studies have found that when businesses are not choosing whether to comply, the optimal deterrence theory fails to work. The effectiveness of punitive regulatory techniques in promoting compliance on the part of ordinary enterprises has been called into question in some recent empirical study. Baldwin comments as follows:

'Corporations…will often be confused and irrational about punitive risks; their staff may conflate individual and corporate liabilities; they may be poorly organized to deal with, anticipate or react to punitive risks and the effects of sanctions; their Boards may under-perform in supervising or providing leadership on punitive risk management and they may be poorly placed to assess how they and their staff are performing as risk managers.'

This presents a variety of questions regarding the connection between risk management, compliance, and deterrent. It reflects the notion that many businesses can be better characterized as organizationally incompetent, with a propensity to uphold the law but with the opportunity for error.

When a company lacks organizational competence, thinking in terms of effective (or credible) deterrence is difficult. The company isn't intentionally breaking the law, therefore it's difficult to stop it. In fact, it is feasible to go even farther and assert that a deterrence strategy is not only likely to be useless in achieving compliance where these enterprises are involved, but also potentially harmful.

One reason for this is that the over-zealous use of enforcement may make firms less inclined to co-operate with regulators. Shapiro and Rabinowitz argue that 'if the government punishes companies in circumstances where managers believe that there has been good faith compliance, corporate officers may react by being less co-operative with regulatory agencies.'

Ayres and Braithwaite provide additional support for this view, suggesting that focusing heavily on formal enforcement is liable to foster 'an organized business subculture of resistance to regulation.' Similar views have been expressed by commentators in a number of different areas.

The use of punishment as a primary tactic may be viewed as "unaffordable, ineffective, and counter-productive in weakening the good will of those with a commitment to compliance." Furthermore, it poses a threat to the cessation of socially beneficial activity since businesses can decide to leave the concerned market.

The second argument against emphasizing deterrence for businesses that lack the desire to violate the law is that doing so is unfair, regardless of the potential consequences. There is a chance that formal sanctions will be applied that do not accurately reflect the firm's guilt.

Even where the formal sanction is a financial penalty, part of the 'sting' of the sanction may be the negative publicity that results from its imposition. The danger of disproportionality is particularly apparent in such circumstances, given that the impact of adverse publicity is determined not formally by the regulator or the courts, but instead by what has been described as the 'capricious jury of public opinion.'

Where the effects of a given enforcement action are excessive, such action will likely (and definitely) be disproportionate. While some critics have suggested that regulators should consider proportionality: 'the most that is required to satisfy the principle of proportionality is formal proportionate quantification of sentence in advance, irrespective of the degree of impact upon an offender.' This is in doubt. It appears difficult to argue that the enforcer has acted proportionately if the regulator anticipates that a specific action is likely to have an unfavorable impact on a specific firm.

3.5.1. Effectiveness of Deterrence Where Firms Are Amoral Calculators

Another issue is that, to the extent that there are rational businesses using a cost-benefit analysis, it is unlikely that these businesses will be discouraged by regulatory actions, whether those actions involve prosecution and the imposition of a (criminal) fine or the imposition of a (civil) financial penalty.

The employment of criminal law, as opposed to civil law, is the main emphasis of the research in this subject. Such studies have emphasized that there is extremely little chance that businesses will be investigated and punished. Looking at regulatory offenses, Ogus estimates that criminal prosecutions account for no more than 0.05% of reported contraventions.

There are several causes for this, but one of them—the resource-intensive nature of prosecution—is one that Macrory emphasizes in Regulatory Justice. The likelihood of being apprehended and subject to official action, such as prosecution, is low, and it is probable that businesses are aware of this.

The value of p is therefore probably low. In addition, where fines are applied, they are normally applied at a modest level (and realized to be so). For example, Macrory quotes the average fine imposed for prosecutions brought by the Environment Agency in 2005 as being just over £5000.

In its major report Changing Banking for Good the Parliamentary Commission on Banking Standards argued that where the FSA's actions against banks were concerned 'the credibility of enforcement has been damaged by a legacy of fines that were pitiful compared to the benefits banks gained from the misconduct.'

Although D includes more than just the formal penalty level (such as the inconvenience of dealing with enforcement action, any negative publicity resulting from such action, and so on), it is unlikely that these additional forms of detriment will be deemed to be significant enough to serve as a credible deterrent. On this basis a rational firm may conclude that the benefits of contravention (U) outweigh the costs.

It may be claimed that when criminal (as opposed to civil) financial fines are involved, the stigma associated with the criminal label gives the penalty more weight. In fact, it has been said that businesspeople “abhor” the stigma associated with criminality.

However, this might be overstated. First, both the public and offenders frequently view regulatory offenses as “not criminal in any true sense.” This suggests that even when members of the public (such as customers) become aware of an offense being committed, they do not significantly stigmatize the offender.

Second, it is unlikely that the general public makes a distinction between a civil or criminal penalty in real-world situations. The term “penalty” is ambiguous in this context, and even “fine” might refer to both criminal and civil pecuniary penalties. Whether a criminal penalty is more likely than a civil sanction to be given publicity (for example by the regulator) is unclear.

When it comes to amoral calculators, the proportionality issue is also important. Every time there is deliberate misbehavior, there can be a case for imposing a penalty. But for that punishment to discourage the amoral calculating, it might need to be so severe as to look out of proportion to the wrongdoing.

In fact, there is a risk of falling into the “deterrence trap,” in which a punishment may be so severe as to force a company out of existence, a result that is sometimes unjustified, in order to serve as an effective deterrent. It can be challenging to strike the right balance between imposing a penalty that is likely to discourage and guaranteeing that any such penalty is not excessive given the transgression.

A further point to consider is that where the process involved does not involve all the safeguards associated with a criminal trial, it may be more likely that mistakes are made. Despite the undoubted safeguards provided in the area of financial services, this remains a concern.

3.5.2. Consequentialism

Finally, the emphasis on deterrence shows that the primary consequentialist principle for penalizing behavior. The FCA seems to think that implementing penalties can result in good things, and that this justifies doing so. This is illustrated, at least to some extent, by some of the principles which underpin the FCA’s approach to its enforcement powers. Principle four states that:

‘The FCA will aim to change the behavior of the person who is the subject of its action, to deter future non-compliance by others, to eliminate any financial gain or benefit from non-compliance, and where appropriate, to remedy the harm caused by non-compliance.' This wording may be familiar to some readers. It reflects the Penalties Principles set out by Macrory in Regulatory Justice. Tracey McDermott, in commenting on the FSA's enforcement in its last year of operation said: 'we have focused on cases where we think we can make a real difference to consumers and markets, using enforcement strategically as a tool to change behavior in the financial services industry.'

The desire of a regulator to concentrate on the results is natural. Focusing on this is usually preferred because the general public expects results from regulators. On the other hand, if that were the only one, that would be worrying.

There are compelling reasons that penalties should be founded, at least in part, on the concept of deserts and that they can also serve as a symbol of rebuke. This may be particularly true of punishments imposed under the criminal law, but it may also be true of other sanctions.

Even while DEPP does include some things that could be characterized as retaliatory or non-consequentialist, the tone of credible deterrence and the focus on consequences appear to be consequential. The more serious the wrongdoing, the more important it is that sanctions reflect that seriousness, regardless of (or in addition to) any aim of achieving deterrence.

Two key components make up seriousness: the type and/or extent of injury, and the degree of blame. A sanctioning system, whether criminal or civil, must be willing to inflict punishments that accurately represent the seriousness of the offense, even when it is unlikely that the behavior would be changed in the future.

3.5.3. Addressing the Concerns

This section looks at how we might address the concerns raised by a focus on credible deterrence. It considers how deterrence might be made more effective; how different types of firms might be treated; how proportionality can be achieved and how sanctioning needs to reflect concepts that might be described as non-consequentialist.

It will become clear that in practice, the FCA does look beyond credible deterrence and address a number of these issues, despite its apparent focus on the concept.

3.5.4. Effectiveness

The first point to consider is the worry that deterrence is unlikely to be credible (and so effective) even for amoral mathematicians. There are several ways to deal with this.

3.5.4.1. Increasing the Value of p

For deterrence tactics to be effective, businesses must first feel that they have a serious chance of being followed, investigated, and punished for misconduct. This is dependent on how the regulator approaches monitoring, specifically in terms of attempting to find violations.

The FCA uses a risk-based strategy, allocating resources in response to dangers that are deemed to exist to its regulatory goals. In relation to its overall approach to supervision, the FCA states:

'The FCA will adopt a pre-emptive approach which will be based on making forward-looking judgments about firms' business models, product strategy and how they run their businesses, to enable the FCA to identify and intervene earlier to prevent problems crystallizing.'

In addition, the FCA has stated that its supervision model is inter alia: 'forward looking and more interventionist...consumer-centric...robust when things go wrong... and viewing poor behavior in all markets through the lens of impact on consumers.' This suggests a qualitatively different attitude to supervision from that taken by its predecessor.

It is conceivable to argue that moving forward, businesses will consider it more probable that wrongdoing will be discovered and addressed given the focus the FCA has stated it concentrates on enterprises (and industries) that potentially hurt consumers or endanger market integrity. In Changing Banking for Good, there is substantial support for placing more emphasis on enforcement action. The Report argues that:

'Greater priority needs to be placed on the role of enforcement, with adequate resources devoted to this function and leadership with a willingness to pursue even the difficult cases, often involving the larger and more powerful players, in order to build up a credible deterrent effect.'

The criteria that the organization will consider when determining whether to pursue financial penalties as part of the FCA's response are outlined in DEPP, however the FCA acknowledges that the list is not all-inclusive and that some won't apply in particular circumstances. The factors are the nature, seriousness, and impact of the suspected breach; the conduct of the person after the breach; the previous disciplinary record and compliance history of the person; FCA guidance and other published materials; action taken by the FSA or FCA in previous similar cases; and action taken by other domestic or international regulatory authorities.

This indicates that deciding whether to apply a penalty is a question of judgment that must be made based on a variety of factors. It also challenges the idea that deterrence is essential to making decisions, as will be seen later.

If deterrence were to become more credible, the FSA had earlier acknowledged the need to express a willingness to act more explicitly. The fact that the FSA issued fewer "fines" (as it called them) in 2012–2013 than it had in any of the two prior fiscal years (FYs) may be cause for concern. Therefore, the emphasis on credible deterrence did not result in a rise in the amount of fines levied.

Despite this decrease, the FCA has made it clear that one of the ways it intends to fulfill its commitment to achieving the consumer protection aim through genuine deterrence is by filing more enforcement cases. It increases the value of p in the model above when this is adequately communicated to those who might consider disobedience.

Even though it is possible that businesses still do not have a precise understanding of what p is worth, this does not make deterrence ineffective. It has been highlighted that for general deterrence to work, how a person perceives the risk of taking on a certain activity is important.

Ogus, for example, suggests that 'if traders generally perceive the value of p to be significantly higher than in reality is the case, there is no reason to disturb this impression if it can contribute to a higher level of compliance.' In practice, it seems unlikely that well-informed firms will consider it more likely that they will face action unless there is in fact an increase.

3.5.4.2. Increasing the Value of D

Second, it must be shown that serious harm is likely to follow where noncompliance is shown for deterrence to be credible. The fine levied as a result of a violation is D's most evident element. When assessing the level of punishment that is suitable and commensurate to the wrongdoing, DEPP outlines some of the considerations to be taken into account.

The regime for penalty setting is based upon three principles: disgorgement, discipline and deterrence. Disgorgement, discipline, and deterrence all refer to the principles that a firm (or individual) should not profit from a breach, that they should be held accountable for any wrongdoing, and that any sanctions should serve as a deterrent to the firm or individual who committed the breach and other parties from committing similar or additional breaches.

Whether the sanctions placed on companies are adequate to support credible deterrence is a tricky question to answer. Since businesses are amoral calculators, as was mentioned earlier, this seems unlikely. However, there is some proof that there has recently been a readiness to strengthen financial sanctions. The FSA imposed £423.2 million in financial penalties during the year 2012–2013.

A compelling case can be made for harsh sanctions, subject to the proportionality concerns presented. Despite the drawbacks of the economic approach to sanctions described above, it appears acceptable to conclude that larger fines are more likely to deter than smaller ones for enterprises that either consciously choose to participate in wrongdoing or who run the danger of doing so.

There remain doubts about whether the financial penalties currently imposed fulfill this, and the question of whether the figures are skewed by action concerning LIBOR is important, but the FCA should receive some credit for the advances that appear to have been made.

It is probable that this will continue because the FCA has stated that it intends to utilize credible deterrence to achieve its consumer protection purpose, including by pursuing more enforcement cases and advocating for harsh penalties for rule violations.

Indeed, Changing Banking for Good argued that both the FCA and the PRA should further review again their penalty setting framework 'to allow for a further substantial increase in fines.'

Perhaps the clearest example of a move towards the imposition of higher financial penalties is the £28 million fine imposed by the FCA upon Lloyds Banking Group (specifically Lloyds TSB Bank plc and Bank of Scotland plc) in December 2013 for serious failings in their controls over sales incentive schemes.

It is the largest ever fine imposed by the FCA or FSA, for failings in retail conduct of business. The FCA investigated advised sales of investment and protection products between 1 January 2010 and 31 March 2012. In their financial incentive programs for their advisers, the firms had "greater risk aspects that were not appropriately regulated," according to the study.

This provided a significant risk that advisers would sell products to customers that they neither needed nor wanted in order to maintain or increase their salaries. Over the period in question, the firms sold £2.25 billion of investment products and received £118 million in protection insurance premiums.

The FCA enhanced the penalties by 10% despite the parties' early settlement agreement (which entitled them to a 20% discount) and the firms' prior disciplinary history. This was due to prior warnings concerning the use of improperly managed incentive programs.

3.5.4.3. Refocusing D

Deterrence tactics are typically discussed in the context of corporate misconduct, and the majority of the discussion above has assumed that a corporation will be the target of a financial punishment. It is notable that the FSA began to focus greater attention on individuals and the FCA has taken this forward. In 2013–2013, the FSA took more actions against individuals than against firms, imposing over £5 million in fines.

It is crucial to pay attention to personal responsibility. Sometimes taking legal action against an individual is preferable to taking legal action against a company. The FCA may take disciplinary action against a "authorized person" where there is evidence of personal responsibility on his or her part, according to DEPP, while acknowledging that the firm is responsible for ensuring compliance with a firm's regulatory requirements.

It continues by saying that 'Personal culpability arises where the behavior was deliberate or where the approved person's standard of behavior was below that which would be reasonable in all the circumstances at the time of the conduct concerned.'

The importance of personal culpability as a deterrence against business misconduct has grown throughout time. A concentration on the firm as a legal person is feared to present unique challenges. First of all, blaming a company for an incident can be challenging.

This is especially true when it comes to criminal law due to the nature of corporate criminal responsibility (where it is notoriously difficult to attach liability for offenses requiring proof of mensrea and may also be problematic where strict liability offenses are accompanied by defense of due diligence).

Fault (universally understood) may exist within companies in different ways and at different levels. The use of criminal law against frequently huge and complicated businesses has been vividly exposed in this regard. For the aim of assigning blame, attempts have been made to document wrongdoing, although it is still challenging to do so.

Second, as was already mentioned, it is debatable whether a monetary fine imposed on a company will have the same deterrent effect as one imposed on an individual. The former may be considered nothing more than a business expense, but the latter (depending on the specific punishment) may result in the person losing not just their means of support but even, in cases where the criminal law is used, their freedom.

Where penalties are administrative rather than criminal, incarceration is not an issue, but loss of livelihood remains so.

The FCA is aware that sometimes a deterrence-based policy would need to focus on specific persons. The FCA specifically stated that it was going to go after senior managers who, in its words, failed to "recognize and manage the risk that their firm is running; regulate the way their goods are offered; and ensure that the interests of consumers are at the core of those designing new products."

This has been reinforced by the FCA's subsequent statements. In June 2013 Tracey McDermott said that 'repeated fines for conduct failures here and overseas demonstrates that fining firms alone is not enough' and that 'we must do something different. In order to achieve credible deterrence, senior managers must be held to account.'

It is argued that the FCA is appropriately concerned with individual fault. The classical criminal law concept of subjective mensrea, which includes ideas like intent, carelessness, and dishonesty, is narrower than fault.

As was already mentioned, there is fault when the approved person behaved in a way that was less than reasonable given the circumstances. This type of objective mistake is crucial because it exemplifies the need for people to consider how their behavior will be perceived from an objective standpoint.

People who don't do it have to deal with personal repercussions. The idea that employees of companies should share part of the blame for the decisions made by those companies has been around for a while. This has primarily appeared in the form of "senior officer" clauses in the criminal law.

Such a senior official is accountable for any crimes committed with his or her knowledge, complicity, or due to any negligence on their part, and is held accountable together with the company. The mention of negligence makes it obvious that there is an objective component to such a provision, even though agreement and connivance entail knowledge of the conditions.

The FCA's emphasis on personal responsibility is to be applauded. Indeed, Changing Banking for Good has pushed for a greater focus on personal accountability. The Report presents several proposals that would give people more responsibility and clarity, and even help deter crime more successfully.

Among these is the suggestion that a 'Senior Persons Regime' replace the Approved Persons Regime in respect of banks. Under this, all the 'key responsibilities' within a bank would be assigned to a specific and senior individual. This, it is suggested, would facilitate the identification of those most responsible for failures and make it easier to use enforcement powers against individuals.

The Report also argues for legislation that would let the FCA and PRA to apply a variety of civil punishments, including a ban, on a person "unless that person can establish that he or she took all reasonable steps to prevent or mitigate the impact of a designated failing."

Two prerequisites must be met for this to be the case: first, the individual's bank must have been the subject of enforcement action that the Tribunal has either settled or upheld, and second, the regulator must be able to demonstrate that the individual held specific responsibilities under the Senior Persons Regime that were directly related to the enforcement action in question.

This is a risky course of action and one that cannot be completely examined here. It is reminiscent to a due diligence defense in criminal law, where the accused is guilty unless they can show they were not at fault. Civil culpability is, however, involved. Furthermore, the Report also recommends the creation of a new criminal offense of reckless misconduct in the management of a bank.

The Report views the offense as offering credible deterrence for individuals who are only covered under the proposed Senior Persons Regime. In its words: 'the fact that recklessness in carrying out professional responsibilities carries a risk of a criminal conviction, and a prison sentence would give pause for thought to the senior officers of UK banks.'

As a civil punishment, significant fines can already be imposed with the benefit of a weaker burden of proof. However, the proposed offense might offer a more powerful deterrent because it carries the potential for incarceration as well as the stigma associated with a conviction.

3.5.4.4. Rethinking D

As was mentioned previously, D comprises more than just the formal penalty because it stands for the harm caused by the violation. D, which stands for the defendant's cost, may also include disruption, inconvenience, and the price of complying with a regulator's post-wrongdoing duties.

Baldwin has emphasized that "penal effects may extend very considerably beyond the level of any fine imposed," implying that formal enforcement action may have a negative impact on reputation, cause operational disruptions and managerial disruptions, deteriorate relationships between regulator and regulated, and have a negative impact on investor relations. Similarly, Ogus recognizes that costs from contravention include:

'The hassle and personal inconvenience arising from encounters with the victims of regulatory contraventions and with public officials, legal, and other defense expenditures, as well as any loss of market reputation resulting from the contravention being detected.'

The potential bad publicity that could result from the violation is one of D's elements that is especially crucial. When a criminal statute has been violated and it has received widespread media attention, the defendant may feel intimidated.

Companies pay great attention to their reputation, which the stigma of a criminal conviction may have a considerable negative impact on. As Ball and Friedman argue: 'the word "crime" has symbolic meaning for the public and the criminal law is stained so deeply with notions of morality and immorality, public censure, and punishment, that labeling an act as criminal often has consequences that go far beyond mere administrative effectiveness.'

They draw the conclusion that "businessmen abhor the concept of being branded a criminal" and that businesspeople are effectively discouraged by fear of legal action. There is little question that businesses that value their public image will be anxious at having the label of criminality linked to them, even though it is suggested that the stigma associated with prosecution and conviction (particularly in the regulatory sector) is frequently overdone.

Not all criminal law violations result in negative publicity. In fact, as was previously mentioned, it is questionable whether the general public can tell the difference between criminal fines and civil financial penalties. As a result, it is likely that at least some negative publicity will result from the widely publicized enforcement of a civil penalty. Concerns may naturally arise if the general public fails to recognize this distinction.

If the word 'crime;' does have symbolic meaning for the public, it is a matter of concern if the public treats noncriminal penalties as carrying the same stigma as criminal penalties.

The FSA also has well-designed punishments that leverage the influence of bad publicity. The FSA has the authority to inflict public censure in addition to financial penalties (which could lead to notoriety in and of themselves).

The FSA's Guidance outlines the variables to be considered when choosing whether to apply a financial penalty or public censure. For example, the first factor is whether deterrence can be achieved effectively through a public censure.

The individual's ability to profit from the breach or to prevent suffering a loss is the second consideration. Seriousness is a third consideration, with monetary sanctions (often) being employed in circumstances involving greater severity. Fourth, public condemnation may be more appropriate if the FSA was informed of the breach by the individual in question.

Fifth, if the offender acknowledges the violation, cooperates completely with the FSA, and takes steps to ensure that individuals who suffer losses receive compensation, this may again favor merely public reprimand. Sixth, a poor record of discipline or compliance is likely to support financial penalties.

Deterrence is given as the justification for this. Seventh, the FSA will strive to establish consistency in its strategy by taking prior cases into consideration. Finally, the FSA will also take into account how the impact will affect the individual.

The considerations show that public reprimand alone will usually be utilized in less serious cases, which may seem surprising considering that bad press may occasionally act as a more powerful deterrent than the implementation of a financial punishment.

Additionally, it should be remembered that unfavorable publicity might develop only by disseminating unfavorable material without the application of a sanction. This is especially clear when it comes to the disclosure of complaint data. Following the publication of aggregate and firm-level data, the FCA mandates companies to submit specific information. Additionally, information regarding the complaints that the financial ombudsman service (FOS) handles is made public. While these would not, typically, be described as sanctions, still less penalties, they may have a chastening effect upon firms and therefore be viewed through the lens of deterrence.

3.5.4.5. From U to D: Removing the Benefits of Contravention

Disgorgement is the first of several guiding concepts on which the FCA's penalty-setting framework is built. This reflects the idea that a company or individual shouldn't profit from any violations of one of Macrory's "Penalties Principles," which is echoed here.

This represents the idea that no one should profit from their crime and is essential to the success of a punishment regime. The benefit from violation is identified as U by the optimal deterrence model. If U can be decreased or abolished, this enhances deterrence and may offer consumers some form of compensation.

Finding more inventive ways to accomplish this has drawn growing interest. The study of consumer redress programs in and of themselves is extremely intriguing. Although discussing these in depth is outside the purview of this chapter, it is noteworthy to highlight the FCA's function in getting redress and its connection to deterrence by citing a recent incident.

In late 2013 the FCA reached an agreement with Card Protection Policy Ltd. (CPP) and 13 high street banks and credit card issuers to pay redress to up to 7 million consumers who were the victims of mis-selling.

CPP had already been fined £10.5 million in November 2012 for failing to treat customers fairly. While some customers were introduced to the goods directly by CPP, others were referred through banks and credit card companies.

If approved by its creditors (a majority the consumers in question who vote) and confirmed by the High Court, this scheme of arrangement could lead to very substantial redress being paid.

It is noteworthy that the Law Commission justified its position that the financial services sector should not be subject to reforms that would give consumers redress for unfair business practices by claiming that "sophisticated mechanisms are already in place to protect consumers" and that redress frequently goes well beyond the types the Law Commission had in mind. The ability to require businesses to create consumer redress programs is a key component of the FCA's responsibility to ensure that consumer redress is properly delivered. However, deterrence is another way to look at such systems.

The FCA can make agreements with businesses since it has the power to impose such a system. As shown in other domains, having powerful enforcement powers frequently makes it possible to negotiate agreements without taking official action.

As the CPP example illustrates, it is possible to combine the imposition of a financial penalty with additional measures which have the effect of operating as a financial penalty, but which are characterized instead as redress. Where this occurs, the deterrent effect may be strong.

3.6. TYPES OF FIRMS AND PROPORTIONALITY

3.6.1. Considering Deterrence Where Intention Is Lacking

As mentioned before, amoral calculators respond best to the notion of optimal deterrence. It assumes that companies decide whether to do wrongdoing and that they ought to be discouraged from doing so. However, many organizations won't be quite so analytical.

It is crucial to think about how much, if at all, credible deterrence affects other firms. First of all, while the FCA has emphasized credible deterrence, it is evident that it considers a range of considerations when determining whether and how to utilize its powers.

A picture of this is provided by the FCA's Enforcement Guide which is produced to describe the FCA's approach to exercising its main enforcement powers. Four main principles underpin the FCA's approach to the use of its enforcement powers, the first three of which emphasize the need not to move immediately to formal enforcement.

First, the FCA admits that having an open and cooperative relationship with those it supervises is crucial to the regime's performance.

Second, the FCA promises to execute its authority in a manner that is "transparent, proportionate, responsive to the issue, and consistent with its publicly stated values." Third, the FCA declares that it would "attempt to ensure equitable treatment while executing its enforcement authorities."

This presents an intriguing contrast to recent statements regarding credible deterrence made by the FCA (and earlier by the FSA). It has always been evident that the regulator must exercise its authority in a reasonable manner, and the Enforcement Guide clarifies what that entails. In reality, regulators are hesitant and even unable to pursue deterrence with the vigor that they occasionally suggest. The approach taken by the majority of regulators does not correspond to optimal deterrence methods of the kind mentioned above.

The reality of regulatory enforcement is that regulators deploy possess, and deploy, a significant amount of bureaucratic discretion. In practice, what have been described as 'compliance strategies' are frequently utilized.

The goal of a compliance strategy, often known as "advise and persuade," is to "ensure conformity with law by securing compliance or by taking action to prevent prospective law violation without the need to detect, process, and penalize violations."

In the words of Hawkins, 'it's conception of enforcement centers upon the attainment of the broad aims of legislation, rather than sanctioning its breach.' As the FCA's comments above demonstrate, compliance-based approaches remain very much in evidence. Where there has been a contravention a judgment has to be made about the appropriate regulatory response.

The FCA advances the normative argument for handling violations without the requirement for formal reprimand or other forms of enforcement. However, it does say that in such cases: 'the FCA will expect the firm to act promptly in taking the necessary remedial action with its supervisors to deal with the FCA's concerns' and that if the firms do not do this disciplinary or other enforcement action may follow.

The 'tit for tat' enforcement method notably supported by Ayres and Braithwaite may be reflected in large part by the FCA's attitude. According to those authors, a strategy like this might be described as follows:

'The regulator refrains from a deterrent response as long as the firm is cooperating; but when the firm yields to the temptation to exploit the co-operative posture of the regulator and cheats on compliance, then the regulator shifts from a cooperative to a deterrent response.'

The FCA is aware of the importance of the firm's mindset, which is heavily emphasized in Tit for Tat. Culture has been discussed a lot recently, both in connection to the regulation and in reference to businesses.

If culture is, as has been suggested, 'the underpinning that drives the decisions we make and the actions we take' it may be reflected in the attitude of a firm to compliance. When viewed in this light, credible deterrence may have a function in discouraging noncooperation and encouraging cooperation.

It's important to keep in mind that there may be (some) responsibility even when no purpose is present. As previously said, a company could have been irresponsible or reckless, or it could have simply allocated insufficient resources to monitoring. Such behavior entails fault and can amount to a corporation breaching many of its commitments.

It could be argued that there remains a role for credible deterrence for contraventions based on carelessness or some other fault falling short of intention or dishonesty. Significant penalties have been imposed on firms for such breaches.

High standards of monitoring by businesses and individuals may be encouraged by the knowledge that a penalty is likely to be levied even for non-intentional infringement. This is one of the arguments for strict liability in criminal law, and it may be especially potent when supported by due diligence defense.

A person will not be found guilty if they can show that even if they committed the actual crime, they took all reasonable precautions and used all due diligence to prevent it. This encourages businesses and people to take precautions to prevent unintended violations.

This will (i) reduce the likelihood that the actus reus will be committed; and (ii) aid to ensure that, should it happen, a defense can be established. Similar to this, organizations, and people who fail to perform their obligations properly may be subject to financial fines on the grounds that doing so will deter future laxity. As a result, even in the absence of intention, credible deterrence may be necessary.

3.7. CONSEQUENTIALIST FOCUS

Another issue with the emphasis on deterrence is that non-consequentialist methods could be overlooked, and their significance lost. Concerns about the degree to which consequentialist theories like deterrence (and rehabilitation) should serve as the foundation for punishment, at least for individuals, have been present at least since the 1960s.

While some observers still maintain these ideas, perhaps attention has switched to the crucial part that punishment plays in reflecting wrongdoing. Theories of punishment based on "just deserts" demanded that punishments not only be final but also be deserving of execution.

It is believed that wrongdoing deserves criticism because it is wrong, and that criticism should represent this wrong. It may be argued that credible deterrence downplays this crucial role for punishments by focusing on potential outcomes rather than actual wrongdoings.

It should be noted that the FCA's regime does recognize, at least to some extent, the importance of non-consequentialist sanctioning. Discipline, or the idea that a company or individual should be punished for misbehavior, is the second principle of the FSA's penalty regime. The constant language of credible deterrence, however, seems to have obscured this.

3.8. CONCLUSION

This chapter summarized credible deterrence and consumer protection through the imposition of financial penalties. Firstly, this chapter discussed the understanding deterrence with definitions and types.

The three essential elements of successful deterrence were discussed in the middle of this chapter, along with some issues with credible deterrence in theory and practice, firm kinds, and disproportionality. The types of firms, proportionality, and, last but not least, an explanation of the consequentialist approach was covered in the chapter's last section.

REFERENCES

1. Cartwright, P., (n.d.). *Credible Deterrence and Consumer Protection Through the …* worktribe.com. Nottingham-repository. Available at: https://nottingham-repository.worktribe.com/index.php/OutputFile/740007 (accessed on 15 June 2023).
2. Mazarr, M. J., (1970). *Understanding Deterrence*. SpringerLink. T.M.C. Asser Press. Available at: https://link.springer.com/chapter/10.1007/978-94-6265-419-8_2 (accessed on 15 June 2023).
3. Mazarr, M. J., (2018). *The Role of Deterrence in U.S. Defense Policy*. RAND Corporation. RAND Corporation. Available at: https://www.rand.org/pubs/perspectives/PE295.html (accessed on 15 June 2023).
4. Mazarr, M. J., (2021). *(PDF) Understanding Deterrence*. researchgate.net. Available at: https://www.researchgate.net/publication/347341312_Understanding_Deterrence (accessed on 15 June 2023).
5. McDermott, T., (2013). *Enforcement and Credible Deterrence in the FCA*. www.fca.org.uk. Thompson Reuters Compliance & Risk Summit. Available at: https://www.fca.org.uk/publication/news/enforcement-credible-deterrence-speech.pdf (accessed on 15 June 2023).

CHAPTER 4

LIBOR Manipulation: The Limits and Potential of Corporate Criminal Liability

Contents

This chapter discusses the limits and potential of corporate criminal liability. At the beginning of this chapter, the chapter explains about the introduction and overview of LIBOR. The chapter also addresses the LIBOR scandal, LIBOR reforms, unintended consequence of the new LIBOR system. The chapter provides the highlights on the corporate liability, the common law rules, and the problem of "Economic Crime."

4.1. INTRODUCTION

The integrity of the London Interbank Offered Rate (LIBOR) came under scrutiny during the height of the subprime mortgage market collapse and the start of the Great Recession (LIBOR).

As one of the foundations of the global financial system, LIBOR is a daily interest rate benchmark based on the interest rates at which banks borrow unsecured funds from other banks in the London wholesale money market (or interbank market) and is used as the base rate in financial transactions valued between an estimated $300 trillion to $800 trillion.

LIBOR affects businesses seeking credit, consumers obtaining mortgages or personal loans, students obtaining educational loans, employees' pension funds, and market participants transacting in numerous other financial contracts in the U.S. and abroad.

Financial media started to notice in 2008 that LIBOR, the most popular reference rate benchmark globally and a leading indication of bank financial soundness, was not as turbulent as one might anticipate given the market upheaval. Several prominent economic indicators that typically have favorable correlations with LIBOR also started to trend in the opposite way.

The difference in interest rates between short-term U.S. government debt and interbank loans, or the "spread" between LIBOR and the TED spread, has historically been small, but has recently started to diverge significantly. Additionally, while some banks' LIBOR submissions stayed the same, their credit default swap rates increased.

Although other leading economic indicators unmistakably indicated that the banks were experiencing significant credit deterioration, the LIBOR submissions of the contributing banks to the British Bankers' Association (BBA), the private organization that oversaw LIBOR until NYSE Euronext took over in January 2014, suggested that borrowing costs remained static during the economic turmoil. On August 12, 2011, a multi-district litigation before the United States District Court for the Southern District of New York was established to address the multiple allegations made against LIBOR contributor banks. At the heart of the litigation was the contention that a cartel of banks had manipulated LIBOR, resulting in billions of dollars of damages to stock market investors, pension funds, community banks, local governments, and participants in the commercial lending and real estate markets.

Banks hurriedly finalized government settlements and fired the traders responsible for the bogus submissions to lessen the pending storm of litigation. However, despite expectations, the legal and financial community's anticipated wave of litigation did not materialize, and as a result, some class action lawsuits were eventually dismissed entirely or in part.

Nevertheless, regulators in the US and the UK continue their long-standing investigations into LIBOR manipulation, and in certain cases have initiated criminal investigations of certain bankers." In 2012, the UK enacted a number of reforms designed to address certain failings in the LIBOR submissions process.

However, it is not yet clear if these changes would stop future benchmark manipulation. The likelihood of future manipulation will remain high in the absence of further changes to the way LIBOR is calculated, including potentially the potential for replacing LIBOR as the main benchmark for international finance.

4.2. OVERVIEW OF LIBOR

Without an understanding of how LIBOR is used in virtually every aspect of daily business transactions, it is impossible to comprehend the breadth of the LIBOR manipulation controversy. LIBOR was formulated in the mid-1980s in response to the development of new market instruments, specifically interest rate swap contracts, foreign currency options and forward rate agreements (Figure 4.1).

Despite offering new investment and expansion options, these new financial instruments necessitated some uniformity in the way market risk was determined. In October 1984, the BBA established the BBA standard for interest rate swaps, or "BBAIRS."

By January 1986, BBAIRS had evolved into what is now LIBOR. Currently, there are over 200 LIBOR panel members, representing 60 nations. Even after the manipulation incident received extensive media coverage, LIBOR is still used as the reference point for the vast majority of financial transactions.

Figure 4.1. LIBOR.

Source: Image by The Blue Diamond Gallery.

It is used in calculating interest rates for everything from business loans, commercial, and residential mortgage loans, investment products in pension funds, derivatives contracts, and money-market funds.

The purpose of LIBOR is to show the interest rate at which big banks can borrow unsecured money from other banks.

Prior to the recent LIBOR reforms, there were 15 various short-term maturities, ranging from overnight to one year, and 10 currencies in which LIBOR was measured, resulting in 150 different LIBOR benchmark rates.

The contributing banks send the interest rate they anticipate paying on an unsecured loan from another bank to Thomson Reuters, the BBA's approved calculation agent, every business day between 11 a.m. and 11:10 a.m. Submissions are secret, and only after Thomson Reuters has published the LIBOR rates in their whole are the rates made public.

When rates are submitted, the top and bottom quartiles are ignored, and the average of the remaining values is used as the LIBOR benchmark rate for that day. For example, with respect to three-month U.S.-dollar LIBOR, 18 banks make up the contributor panel that determines the benchmark rate.

In order to eliminate outliers from the calculating process, the top and bottom quartiles are excluded. Only 10 banks' combined data are used to determine the three-month U.S.-dollar LIBOR at any given moment after the upper and bottom quartiles of submitted rates are disregarded. Once published, the LIBOR rate is used to set interest rates on transactions in the lending, securities, derivatives, and currency markets. 's Lenders use LIBOR in pricing loans, adding an increment designed to capture the risk of default by the borrower.

Global markets were significantly affected by contributor banks' collusion to artificially establish the LIBOR benchmark rate. This may have been done to protect their reputations during the financial crisis or to benefit from their positions in certain financial transactions.

The LIBOR crisis is a result of financial institutions and individual traders having built-in incentives to manipulate LIBOR. The capacity to manipulate the LIBOR benchmark rate, even by the smallest fractions of a basis point, could, in some circumstances, cause both borrowers and lenders to make significant overpayments or underpayments.

Borrowing banks (and other borrowers throughout the integrated financial system) benefit from lower rates, while lending banks (and other lenders throughout the integrated financial system) benefit from higher rates.

Positions on derivatives contracts held by specific contributing banks may have influenced banks to manipulate the benchmark rate. The divergence of LIBOR marks against other economic indicators that typically correlated favorably with LIBOR suggested that contributing banks were manipulating their LIBOR marks up or down to appear more financially stable than they actually were because LIBOR is a measure of a contributing bank's financial health.

These fraudulent marks may have had a considerable influence on international markets and market players due to the contributing banks' capacity to manipulate LIBOR.

Individual traders with performance-based compensation had personal motivations to manipulate LIBOR rates to reach financial targets during periods of regular market activity, outside of maintaining a bank's public perception of financial soundness in times of market turbulence.

4.2.1. Commercial and Mortgage Lending

The main component of commercial and mortgage lending is LIBOR. Commercial banks have switched from employing long-term fixed-rate loans to variable-rate loans based on LIBOR to protect themselves from market risks when issuing certain loans, such as construction loans, floating rate bridge loans, and mini-permanent financing. Commercial loans typically have interest rates that are "spread" over LIBOR and that reset frequently throughout the loan's term. Due to manipulation of the LIBOR benchmark, even a tiny increase of a 100th of a percentage point in the interest rate can have a considerable impact on the amount that commercial debtors pay.

In contrast, any decline in LIBOR indicates that a sizable portion of commercial loans was mispriced, leading in poorer returns for lenders. For example, an estimated 7,000 small and medium-sized banks lost approximately $448 million in total revenue due to understated LIBOR marks.

LIBOR is also used to determine certain borrowing rates for consumers and corporations with respect to approximately $10 trillion in commercial and residential mortgage loans. So Approximately 9,00,000 outstanding residential home loans originated between 2005 and 2009 – the period of suspected LIBOR manipulation-totaling approximately $275 billion in outstanding principal.

And over the last decade, an estimated 12 million or more adjustable-rate mortgage (ARM) loans originated in the U.S., totaling over $3.5 billion. If these LIBOR-indexed ARM loans were manipulated in any way, the interest that the borrowers may have paid may have exceeded what they should have.

On the other hand, if LIBOR linked interest rates were driven lower, ARM mortgagees would have most likely paid less than the acceptable market rate. Even a small change in interest rates might result in billions of dollars in losses for both mortgagees and mortgagors in a market worth trillions of dollars.

4.2.2. Financial Market Impact

LIBOR affects the stock market in three fundamental ways:

- The pricing of LIBOR serves as a signal to investors about the perceived health of particular banks, which may have an impact on the prices of the corresponding stocks;
- It serves as the basis for determining the interest rate on LIBOR-based securities, including money-market funds and short-term bonds; and finally.
- LIBOR is used in setting the costs relating to the futures and interest rate swap markets.

First, by inflating LIBOR rates, banks gave the impression that their internal finances were in better shape than they were by reporting borrowing costs that were lower than their actual borrowing costs. In order to reassure investors, governmental regulators, and counterparties that there was no issue with the interbank lending market, LIBOR contributor banks believed that market turmoil created incentives to lower LIBOR submissions. These findings are based on documents made public as part of the Barclays PLC (Barclays) settlement.

These artificially lower LIBOR submissions by certain contributor banks pressured other contributor banks to do the same.

For instance, the management of Barclays thought that the artificially lower LIBOR submissions made by the other contributing banks caused market observers and the media to believe that Barclays had liquidity issues because the LIBOR rate it submitted was significantly higher than the rates made by other banks.

It was claimed that senior management at Barclays instructed the traders in charge of making LIBOR submissions to make lower submissions in order to align Barclays' submissions with those of the other contributor banks. As a result, between 2005 and 2009, Barclays submitted altered LIBOR rates for multiple tenors on a regular basis (Figure 4.2).

Figure 4.2. Financial market.

Source: Image by The Blue Diamond Gallery.

It is possible that the adjustment itself had an impact on investors' decisions about where to direct their banking operations and which bank stocks to buy and sell. Contributing banks who were punished for LIBOR manipulation have seen their individual stock prices face substantial market drops after the reported settlements. Numerous money-market funds and short-term bonds are impacted by LIBOR, second. Because of this, LIBOR tampering would have influenced the interest rate paid on and the market value of such investments.

An investor in a money-market fund indexed to LIBOR, for instance, would have earned less interest if LIBOR had been manipulated downward, and the market value of any outstanding bonds indexed to LIBOR would have fallen if LIBOR had been manipulated upward (as the market value of a bond tends to move inversely to subsequent changes in the relevant interest rate).

Finally, market participants are impacted by interest rate hedges that these market players sign to safeguard themselves against future swings in interest rates based on LIBOR in addition to probable greater or lower payments from investments in LIBOR-indexed financial products.

Interest rate swap products frequently use LIBOR for determining pricing. Any mispricing of LIBOR would necessarily result in the mispricing of interest rate swap contracts as well.

4.2.3. Market Confidence

The banking industry's reputation was badly harmed by the subprime mortgage crisis and subsequent taxpayer-funded bailouts. The LIBOR scandal, which has the potential to further undermine market participants' already weakened confidence in the financial sector, is a crisis at the core of the financial system.

Participants in the financial market use LIBOR as an established framework for a range of financial operations. Because of this, it's possible that investors and financial institutions all across the world have been influenced by the common belief that LIBOR is a poor benchmark.

Over the past five years, since market watchers began to suspect that LIBOR was being manipulated, investors have withdrawn over $500 billion dollars in investments from the equity markets and the number of investors that state they have reduced faith in the functioning of the stock market has more than doubled.

Many LIBOR contributor institutions are debating whether to continue participating in the LIBOR process in light of the heightened regulation and internal reforms, or possibly because of them. In February 2013, U.K. regulators warned both BNP Paribas and Rabo bank not to relinquish their membership as LIBOR contributor banks. There are a number of reasons why banks that contribute to LIBOR might think about exiting the LIBOR panel. The ability of banks to assess the risk of default when deciding whether to provide loans to other banks has been weakened by the lack of confidence in the LIBOR process itself.

Potential market instability is heightened by a lack of liquidity among banks. In addition, LIBOR panel members are worried about their responsibility if they are connected to the settlement process, regardless of whether they were directly involved in the scam.

The net effect is that, in a world where confidence in the honesty of regulators and financial actors is essential for a functioning market, investors, and financial actors alike have less faith in the banking system.

4.3. THE LIBOR SCANDAL

On June 27, 2012, Barclays admitted to regulators in the U.S. and the U.K. that its traders had manipulated the LIBOR benchmark rate for a four-year period beginning as early as 2005 Barclays agreed to pay approximately $435 million in fines to U.S. and U.K. authorities and to cooperate with U.S. and U.K. authorities in their continuing investigations.

Soon after, on December 19, 2012, Swiss bank, UBS AG (UBS), and its subsidiary, UBS Securities Japan Co., Ltd. (UBS Japan), were fined approximately $1.2 billion for their role in LIBOR manipulation by the U.S. Department of Justice (DOJ) and the Commodities and Futures Trading Commission (CFTC), approximately $259.2 million by the U.K.'s Financial Services Authority (FSA), and approximately $64.3 million by Swiss banking authorities.

Royal Bank of Scotland (RBS) became the third major international bank to settle claims of LIBOR manipulation, settling for £87.5 million ($147 million) with U.K. regulatory authorities, $325 million with the CFTC, and $150 million with the DOJ to resolve the investigations.

All other LIBOR contributors are the subject of an investigation by several foreign agencies into possible manipulation of LIBOR or other relevant benchmarks. Affected parties started standalone and class action lawsuits against the alleged conspirator banks while governments around the world launched new investigations or maintained their ongoing probes into the LIBOR scam. In the Southern District of New York, many class action cases alleging LIBOR manipulation by banking companies were recently rejected. It is yet unclear how much this dismissal will impede or affect further litigation.

Within a year of Barclays' settlement with U.S. and U.K. authorities, recommended reforms had been issued and were being implemented by U.K. authorities. This was made possible by the rush on the part of governmental authorities and LIBOR contributor banks to resolve charges of LIBOR manipulation.

However, it is uncertain if the reforms made to the LIBOR calculating method would shield LIBOR against manipulation in the future.

Inconsistencies in the determination of short-term interest rates were first noted by financial observers in late 2007, particularly with regard to the derivatives markets. LIBOR fluctuates based on market predictions for future interest rates, the liquidity cost for lending, and the cost of providing credit.

Financial analysts also pointed out differences in interest rates between EURIBOR benchmarks, the rates European banks established for lending to one another, and LIBOR benchmarks, the rates banks anticipated to make on unsecured loans.

The LIBOR and EURIBOR rates typically move in the same market direction, both theoretically and practically. However, beginning in 2007, along with the upheaval in the subprime market and the collapse of Lehman Brothers, bankers, and interest-rate swap traders started to notice a divergence between the LIBOR and EURIBOR benchmark rates: LIBOR rates moving downward, and EURIBOR rates moving upward.

Banking analysts also noted that the difference between LIBOR and the TED spread was evidence that financial institutions were concealing solvency difficulties. The use of Benford's Law to analyze the LIBOR submissions, which is frequently employed as a technique for detecting fraud, also seemed to point to manipulation of the benchmark.

In September 2007, the financial press started publishing their suspicions regarding the abuse of the LIBOR benchmark. The "smoking gun" for financial reporters was the sudden divergence between reported LIBOR benchmarks and the cost of credit-default swaps.

At the same time, banking authorities and business insiders started publicly challenging the LIBOR benchmarks based on market data at meetings of bond trading associations (and even in government publications) after Bear Steams collapsed.

4.3.1. Governmental Investigations and Litigations

The LIBOR scandal is already global in nature: governmental investigations are ongoing in the United States, the United Kingdom, Canada, the European Union, Switzerland, and Japan. The DOJ, SEC, CFTC, and seven other international regulatory agencies have resolved investigations or are continuing to investigate more than a dozen banks on the nature and extent of LIBOR manipulation.

To date, Barclays, Citigroup, Credit Suisse, Deutsche Bank, JPMorgan Chase, RBS, Bank of America, The Bank of Tokyo-Mitsubishi UFJ, Lloyds TSB, HSBC, Rabobank, Royal Bank of Canada, West LB, Norinchukin, and UBS have either settled claims of LIBOR manipulation, or they continue to be under investigation by regulatory authorities.

In August 2007, a Barclays employee sent a single email that served as the catalyst for the investigations into LIBOR fixing. The email was widely disseminated by the whistleblower, notably among Federal Reserve Bank of New York officials (FRBNY).

The whistleblower mentioned in the email that LIBOR contributions were less than the rates at which the participating LIBOR banks could really borrow. Through the rest of the year, more bulk emails were sent out reporting lower-than-anticipated LIBOR benchmarks.

In response to these emails, FRBNY analysts started to concentrate on the LIBOR benchmarks and started speaking with Barclays staff members. One of these workers claimed to the FRBNY researchers that the lower LIBOR rates were a direct reaction to the bad press that the submission of "honest LIBOR" benchmarks had generated.

By mid- to late-2008, regulatory authorities in the U.S. and U.K. were aware of the industry concerns regarding LIBOR.' Prior to looking into the behavior of the banks, regulator activity was first centered solely on improving the LIBOR filing procedure. However, no progress was achieved in streamlining the LIBOR computation procedure.

The main effort at the time had to be on regaining industry trust in LIBOR due to worries about the stability of the financial system. In June 2008, Timothy Geithner, then-President of the FRBNY, emailed a list of recommendations to Mervyn King, then-Governor of the Bank of England. Geithner's email proposed a number of changes to the LIBOR settlement process, including the following:

- The LIBOR calculation process should be subject to a new and credible reporting process;
- The number and size of U.S. dollar LIBOR contributors should be expanded;
- Incentives should be added to eliminate the misreporting of LIBOR;
- A second calculation time should be added for U.S. dollar LIBOR for the U.S. market;
- The transaction size for each of the LIBOR contributing banks' individual LIBOR marks should be made public; and
- Banks that participate in LIBOR should disclose any LIBOR maturities that benefit the connected reporting bank financially.

The BBA's response to Geithner's recommendation was not very enthusiastic; the organization just released a consultation paper for its members to evaluate and freely implement.

Although there were numerous signs on the market that LIBOR manipulation was prevalent, U.S. and U.K. officials continuously refused to look into the matter or make any effort to stop it. Regulators also did not do much to stop the manipulation after the initial probe.

4.4. EXAMPLE OF THE LIBOR SCANDAL

There are several ways in which the LIBOR scandal's influence may have been felt, even though it is difficult to determine whether any one person was impacted. For example, individual homeowners may have initiated fixed-rate mortgages at a time when mortgage rates were artificially lifted based on upward manipulation of the LIBOR.

From the standpoint of the homeowner, every dollar in extra costs brought on by the inflated rates could be considered as a form of "theft" by the LIBOR rate fixers. Like how many traders who participated in derivative contracts would have unnecessarily suffered significant losses as a result of the LIBOR affair.

The LIBOR scandal left many changes in its wake. Following the exposure of the LIBOR collusion, Britain's Financial Conduct Authority (FCA) took the responsibility for LIBOR supervision away from the British Bankers Association (BBA) and turned it over to the Intercontinental Exchange's Benchmark Administration (IBA).

The IBA is an independent U.K. subsidiary of the private U.S.-based exchange operator, Intercontinental Exchange (ICE). LIBOR is now commonly known as ICE LIBOR.

The FCA recently declared that it will only continue to support LIBOR through 2021, after which it intends to switch to a different methodology. In April 2018, the New York Federal Reserve introduced the secured overnight financing rate (SOFR), a potential LIBOR substitute that is based on short-term loans seen in the repo market.

Unlike the LIBOR, there's extensive trading in Treasury repos – roughly 1,500 times that of interbank loans as of 2018—theoretically making it a more accurate indicator of borrowing costs. Moreover, the SOFR is based on data from observable transactions rather than on estimated borrowing rates, as is sometimes the case with LIBOR.

An interest rate that is fixed and maintained over the course of the loan's term is known as a fixed-rate mortgage. Homeowners may easily create budgets because even though the monthly principal and interest payments vary from payment to payment, the overall payment does not.

The partial amortization schedule below shows how the amounts contributed to principle and interest change throughout the course of the mortgage. In this example, the mortgage term is 30 years, the principal is $1,00,000, and the interest rate is 6%.

The principal benefit of a fixed-rate loan is that it protects the borrower from abrupt and potentially considerable increases in monthly mortgage payments in the event that interest rates rise. Fixed-rate mortgages are simple to comprehend and rarely differ between lenders.

The disadvantage of fixed-rate mortgages is that, during periods of high interest rates, getting approved for a loan might be more challenging due to the lower affordability of the payments. The effect of various rates on your monthly payment can be shown to you using a mortgage calculator.

4.5. LIBOR REFORMS

4.5.1. The Wheatley Report

Following the settlement by Barclays, the U.K. Treasury appointed Martin Wheatley, the managing director of the FSA, to review the LIBOR settlement process and evaluate potential options for reforming the LIBOR system. On September 28, 2012, the "Wheatley Report" was issued.

In lieu of completely doing away with LIBOR as a benchmark, the report presented a 10-point strategy for improving the LIBOR system right away. The 10-point plan of the Wheatley Report can be broken down into three major areas of reform:

- Increasing regulation of LIBOR and providing for criminal sanctions in the case of manipulation;
- Strengthening the governance and oversight of the LIBOR settlement process; and
- Strengthening the LIBOR mechanism with immediate reforms to the LIBOR settlement process.

First, the Wheatley Report suggested the creation of new criminal and civil sanctions for the manipulation or attempted manipulation of LIBOR because these actions were not covered by the Financial Services and Market Act 2000 (FSMA). This would have been the first time that LIBOR manipulation was included in the category of market abuse.

The FSMA, which gives the FSA the authority to pursue specific criminal offenses, was examined by the Wheatley Report in its current shape. In particular, Section 397 of the FSMA allowed the FSA to prosecute parties for misleading statements and practices.

However, the Wheatley Report concluded that the manipulation and attempted manipulation of LIBOR (or any other benchmarks) would not constitute an offense under Section 397 of the FSMA because the deceptive claims or actions had to be conducted with the intent to induce someone to perform particular actions in connection with certain agreements or investments, or with reckless disregard for the possibility that such an outcome might occur.

As a result, the Wheatley Report came to the conclusion that it was unlikely that Section 397 of the FSMA would apply to any manipulation or attempted manipulation of LIBOR submissions because the LIBOR manipulation affected already-existing contracts or was carried out to prevent bad press about the offending party's liquidity.

Accordingly, the Wheatley Report recommended that the U.K. Parliament amend Section 397 of the FSMA to address benchmark manipulation.

Second, the Wheatley Report included many suggestions meant to fortify the organizations in charge of overseeing the LIBOR process. The Wheatley Report suggested that a new and independent private administrator be chosen via an open procurement procedure in light of the BBA's close relationships to the LIBOR contributing banks. In order to improve transparency, the new administrator would be responsible for:

- Collecting and distributing LIBOR submissions; and
- Scrutinizing LIBOR contributor banks to guarantee the integrity of their LIBOR submissions.

In addition to the new administrator, the Wheatley Report also recommended the establishment of an independent oversight committee, which would verify LIBOR submissions via input from additional market participants.

All parties involved in the LIBOR settlement process would be subject to a new code of conduct that would be developed by this new oversight group. The new code of conduct would formalize the LIBOR setting procedure and set up internal measures to stop LIBOR manipulation in the future.

To increase transparency, the new oversight committee would also publish the names of LIBOR contributor members, their declared conflicts of interests, and the minutes of any meetings.

The Wheatley Report also suggested a number of quick changes that would help to rebuild public trust in the LIBOR submission procedure. The Wheatley Report suggested delaying publishing of all LIBOR submissions for a minimum of three months to restrict member banks' ability to foresee LIBOR submissions and, thus, lower the likelihood of manipulation.

The Wheatley Report underlined that contributor banks should take real transactions into account when computing their LIBOR submissions to boost transparency and strengthen the process' integrity. Examples of this transactional information include intervals between transactions and times of transaction submission.

4.5.2. Legislative and Market Reforms

As the LIBOR contributor banks, lawyers, and litigants struggle with lawsuits and legal settlements over damages resulting from LIBOR manipulation, U.K. regulatory authorities and the BBA have moved to enact portions of the Wheatley Report. The Wheatley Report proposals were enacted in order to:

- Reform the LIBOR calculation process itself;
- Prevent related future market calamity; and
- Restore market confidence.

On April 1, 2013, the Financial Services Act 2012 went into effect, which replaced the FSA in early 2014 with a new regulatory body, the FCA. The FCA's goals are to encourage healthy competition in the financial services sector and to safeguard the interests of consumers.

The FCA has the authority to temporarily interfere in the financial markets in order to halt already-in-use financial products or to prevent the launch of new financial products. The FCA can demand that businesses immediately withdraw or modify any deceptive financial marketing if doing so will benefit consumers. The FCA will publicize its enforcement proceedings against companies for violating or failing to comply with financial rules.

Following the recommendations of the Wheatley Report, the Financial Services Act 2012 has amended certain provisions of the FSMA in order to address the actions of traders and bankers with respect to the LIBOR scandal. First, the Financial Services Act 2012 amended Section 22 and Schedule 2 of the FSMA to include benchmark-related activities as "regulated activities" under the FSMA.

Section 397 of the FSMA has expressly been modified with new provisions that address the charge of making false representations that give impressions connected to benchmarks. The new provision criminalizes the following:

- Somebody who intentionally or carelessly communicates a false or misleading statement to another with the goal of establishing a meaningful standard;
- Anyone who intentionally or negligently creates a false or misleading impression about the pricing of an investment or transaction with an interest rate that could influence the setting of a relevant benchmark through their actions is prohibited.

At present, LIBOR is the only benchmark specifically subject to this new provision. All banks that contribute to LIBOR are subject to FCA reviews of their LIBOR systems and procedures. As part of the changes, the FCA mandates that banks name a representative who will oversee ensuring that the new LIBOR processes are followed. This representative must be approved by the FCA.

Any time a benchmark is found to have been manipulated or has been attempted to be manipulated, the FCA rules compel the new LIBOR compliance officer to promptly notify the FCA. Banks who contribute to LIBOR will also put new internal policies and processes in place to stop future manipulation. These new policies include:

- Establishing an internal code of conduct relating to appropriate LIBOR submissions;
- Appointing an oversight committee to administer and review LIBOR submissions;
- Creating a process for managing conflicts of interest relating to LIBOR submissions;
- Keeping a five-year record of all LIBOR submissions; and
- Appointing an independent auditor that will review the bank's compliance procedures and make annual reports to the FCA.

4.6. UNINTENDED CONSEQUENCES OF THE NEW LIBOR SYSTEM

While the Wheatley Report improvements that have been put into place and the shift in who controls the LIBOR-setting process may increase transparency, it is unclear whether these adjustments will actually be able to stop future manipulation or regain market trust in the LIBOR calculating process.

The modifications that have been put into place may have unforeseen negative effects or may not increase clarity in the LIBOR calculating process are covered in this portion of this chapter. Specifically, this section of the chapter will review the following reforms:

- the discontinuation of certain tenors from the LIBOR calculation process;
- the mechanisms used to tie LIBOR to actual transaction costs;
- the transfer of LIBOR oversight from the BBA to NYSE Euronext; and
- the three-month period of confidentiality before the public release of LIBOR benchmarks.

This section of the chapter will analyze each of these particular modifications to the LIBOR procedure and then suggest any more reforms or adjustments that are required to achieve the objectives of improved transparency and certainty in the LIBOR methodology.

4.6.1. Discontinued Currencies and Tenors

A considerable drop in a number of LIBOR currencies and tenors that had little to no value on international markets or were excessively difficult to assess in relation to actual market rates was suggested by the Wheatley Report.

The Wheatley Report's authors sought to shift market participants into tenors with significant market activity by doing away with these LIBOR calculations, which would lead to fewer rate quotes and higher accuracy in terms of actual market costs.

As a result, the BBA has discontinued eight LIBOR tenors: the two-week, four-month, five-month, seven-month, eight-month, nine-month, 10 month, and 11-month tenors. In addition, the BBA has stopped quoting LIBOR in the following currencies and indexes: Canadian dollars, Australian dollars, New Zealand dollars, Swedish krona, Danish krone, and the sterling repo index.

There are a number of unfavorable effects that may affect market participants, even while the goal of discontinuing certain currencies and tenors may be to improve efficiency and reduce submissions in tenors that are challenging to confirm.

First, it is likely that changes will need to be made to the contractual paperwork for ongoing transactions that are connected to these current tenors. When LIBOR becomes unavailable, this may never be a problem for those parties with well-prepared agreements if the underlying transaction documents already call for the use of an alternate reference rate.

However, it is unclear how much the parties had planned for alternate benchmarks in their documents prior to the LIBOR crisis becoming widely known. As a result, the expense of further negotiations and due investigation may be incurred to convert to a new standard.

Moreover, with respect to certain market participants, counterparties may interpret any change to the LIBOR benchmark in their documents as a materially adverse effect, allowing counterparties to select whether to honor contractual obligations. As a result, certain market participants fear that the LIBOR reforms risk invalidating their contracts.

Market participants impacted by these developments have so far been given a number of unsatisfactory options by industry groupings. It has been proposed that market participants choose the "closest" surviving tenor for such contracts when the tenor previously employed has been removed.

For those market participants using LIBOR set to terminated currencies, the suggested options are rather stark: agree to a substitute rate or terminate the transactions entirely.

4.6.2. Setting Libor to Actual Market Rates

The Wheatley Report proposed that market participants utilize a new or revised benchmark based on actual lending data to establish LIBOR in order to regain market participants' confidence in the banking system and the LIBOR calculation process. As part of a new LIBOR calculation process, the FCA requires LIBOR contributor banks to confirm LIBOR's correlation with other financial data.

Theoretically, market players might borrow and lend money at fair and accurate pricing if LIBOR was set to correlate to statistics. However, this raises two fundamental questions: (i) what are "actual market rates;" and (ii) how are these actual market rates collected and calculated?

It is currently unknown what specific modifications NYSE Euronext, as the new LIBOR manager, may demand of banks when setting up LIBOR. However, NYSE Euronext has stated that it will demand that future LIBOR estimates be "anchored" to actual market rates. Market watchers have suggested several options for tying LIBOR to real market costs.

For example, it is recommended that contributor banks use the overnight index swap rate, which reflects the overnight rate at which banks lend to each other, as a data set for LIBOR calculations. Alternatively, banks also could utilize rates used for short-term secured financing between banks and commercial borrowers.

Banks have reacted differently to these proposals. The opposition to this shift by the contributing banks has drawn criticism from some financial commentators as being questionable. The fact that it can be challenging to base market pricing for lending in some tenors on real transactions in some circumstances, however, is a shortcoming of this approach.

The Wheatley Report and other FCA reforms have made an effort to solve this issue by getting rid of tenors and currencies that have little to no market impact. However, in times of significant volatility or in some markets with little to no activity, linking LIBOR to real market rates may become troublesome.

In addition, moving to actual market data may create market disruptions while contributor banks create a consensus on the new market methodologies for a reality-based LIBOR. One solution is to make LIBOR benchmarks contingent, rather than based, on actual market data.

LIBOR submissions might simply be dependent on the existence of actual trade data, as opposed to creating a "Frankenstein" benchmark from a variety of transaction data. This could include further banning any tenors or currencies where there are no markets or trading, which has its own unforeseen effects.

It appears fair that this prospective reform be the duty of NYSE Euronext working with the LIBOR panel banks because it necessitates considerable understanding of the markets and kinds of transactions that rely on LIBOR benchmarks.

4.7. CORPORATE LIABILITY

The phrase "corporate liability" refers to the legal procedures that allow businesses to be held accountable for misconduct as independent legal entities from their owners, officers, or workers. In all of the legal systems of the United Kingdom, the idea of corporation liability is well-established.

Based on the vicarious responsibility principles, corporate liability for wrongs committed by a company's workers or agents has been firmly established in civil law for at least 200 years. Organizations may be held legally responsible for financial losses suffered by an individual or a group of individuals as a result of actions made on the organization's behalf.

Additionally, it is well-established that businesses may be held criminally liable under the strict liability doctrine for violating a legal obligation embodied in legislation designed to control particular fields of business and industry, such as licensing laws or regulations governing workplace health and safety.

Except where there is statutory provision, such as the Corporate Manslaughter and Corporate Homicide Act 2007, the attribution of corporate criminal liability for serious mainstream offending is governed by common law rules.

Common law in this context is law derived from judgments in individual cases rather than written in statute. The identification theory is a set of common law principles that govern corporate liability for economic crimes, such as fraud and false accounting, committed by employees or others who are authorized to represent the organization.

The one exception to the applicability of the common law rules in the area of economic crime is the offense of a corporate failure to prevent bribery at Section 7 of the Bribery Act 2010. Evidence that the common law standards on corporate responsibility and regulatory fines were failing to address commercial bribery led to the creation of this offense.

Since its implementation in July 2011 Section 7 has provided a powerful incentive for the inclusion of bribery prevention procedures as a component of corporate good governance. Its utility as an enforcement tool has been recently demonstrated.

4.7.1. The Issue to Be Addressed

Major corporate malfeasance has occurred recently. Focus has been placed on misbehavior in the financial services industry, but not just by the media and the general public. The response of the UK authorities has been to apply both regulatory and criminal law. Companies have been subject to fines and individuals imprisoned.

In certain instances, the proof of wrongdoing was insufficient to support a criminal case against a business under the identification concept. There are several opinions on how this will affect things. A problem to bringing successful criminal corporation charges, according to some analysts, is the identification concept.

This doctrine requires prosecutors to prove that those who can be regarded as "the directing mind" of the company knew about, actively condoned or played a part in the offending. The government is interested in determining the degree to which the identification theory may be impeding efficient criminal law enforcement and developing reform ideas as appropriate.

In doing so, it is crucial to assess the significance of any failures in light of the overall Government's past efforts to combat misbehavior.

4.7.2. Wider Government Action

Criminal charges are simply one of the tools available to deter behavior and hold people accountable; in particular, industries and for certain types of behavior, criminal consequences coexist with regulatory enforcement measures and fines. For example, the Competition and Markets Authority promotes open competition among companies for the benefit of consumers.

FCA and Prudential Regulatory Authority (PRA) are the organizations in charge of overseeing the financial services industry (PRA). That system aims to encourage regulated financial organizations to practice good governance. The governance of companies more generally, including the duties placed on Directors, is addressed by the Companies Act 2006 and the Financial Reporting Council's Corporate Governance Code. The UK Anti-Corruption Plan, published in December 2014, tasked the Ministry of Justice to examine the case for a new offense of a corporate failure to prevent economic crime and the rules on establishing corporate criminal liability more widely.

Due to the lack of enforcement action testing of the Bribery Act failure to prevent model and the lack of proof of corporate misbehavior going unpunished, that effort was discontinued in the summer of 2015.

4.7.3. The Consultation Process

Research to propose expanding the Bribery Act failure to prevent model offense to a wider variety of economic crimes was announced by the then-Prime Minister at the Anti-Corruption Summit on May 12, 2016, in response to these developments. This chapter is published in pursuance of that announcement.

It focuses on obtaining data regarding the scope of the issue, knowledge regarding the key concerns raised, and opinions on the case for reform choices, including the failure to prevent model. Although it is published for general consumption, it will be especially pertinent to businesses and other corporate entities having legal personality, academics, civil society, and the legal profession.

4.8. THE COMMON LAW RULES

4.8.1. Corporate and Unincorporated Bodies and Partnerships

In accordance with common law, only "corporate bodies" are capable of committing crimes. This is so that businesses can be regarded "legal persons" in their own right since they are typically formed through the legal process of "incorporation," which grants them a legal identity distinct from the people who form, own, or control them.

This distinguishes them from most forms of "partnership" and "unincorporated bodies." Partnerships are recognized in common law and in statute and provide a framework in which individual partners engaged in the same profession are able to pool resources and share any liability arising from their activities.

Many partnerships lack a distinct legal identity from their members and are therefore not regarded as "legal persons" under common law. According to Scottish law, a partnership (or firm) may be sued independently of its individual participants because it has its own legal identity. Unincorporated bodies, which are typically associations representing a group of people involved in a certain activity and lack a legal existence distinct from the members, are not regarded as "legal persons" for the purposes of the common law.

4.8.2. The Development of the Identification Doctrine

Companies swiftly grew to play a vital part in our economy and culture after emerging as a Middle Ages vehicle of commercial convenience. As a result, the courts have long held that corporate activity should be criminalized and that the law should offer individuals recourse against the unwarranted exercise of corporate authority.

Since the passage of the Interpretation Act 1889 (now known as the Act of 1978), the term "person" used in any criminal legislation is to be understood as referring to both an individual and a group of people, whether they be corporate or unincorporated.

There must be a way to link the actions of workers or agents in committing the crime to the company for it to be found guilty. If the crime also calls for it, the employees' or agents' mental condition must also be linked to the firm. It has taken a while for legal tools to be created to accomplish this.

During the 19th century the courts came to recognize limited corporate criminal liability for a narrow range of offenses that included public nuisance, criminal libel, and breach of statutory duty.

Although vicarious responsibility was recognized in civil law as a legal theory for holding an organization accountable for the actions of its workers or agents, it has not been recognized in the UK as a legal theory for holding an organization criminally liable. This contrasts with the position in the United States where the civil law vicarious liability doctrine of respond eat Superiore has been extended to the criminal law.

4.8.3. The Leading Case

In the leading case of Tesco Supermarkets Ltd v Nattrass, the House of Lords ruled that the attribution of corporate criminal liability for offenses requiring proof of criminal intent is governed by a doctrine of general application applied without reference to the legislative context of the offense.

It was accepted that businesses operated via live individuals, and that an individual who was correctly identified would speak or act on behalf of the business rather than on its behalf. However, this would only apply if the individual were the one in charge of the organization's direction.

In his leading opinion, Lord Diplock took the view that in order to determine the scope of the persons, the acts and state of mind of whom can be attributed to the company, one need only look to the company's memorandum of association, i.e., the board of directors, the managing director, and possibly other superior officers of the company.

In many circumstances, the prohibited act or omission will be committed by people who are not located at the corporate center, as acknowledged by the logic for the judgment. When that occurs, a person who is legitimately recognized as the company's controlling mind and will must have the necessary purpose for the company to be found guilty of the crime for the corporation to be prosecuted.

The emphasis on a proper reading of the legislation in determining the attribution of corporate liability returned in the Privy Council case of Meridian Global Funds Management Asia Ltd v Securities Commission in 1995.

According to Lord Hoffman's leading opinion, the Tesco and Nattrass directing mind test should be viewed by the courts as one attribution rule that, if applied arbitrarily, might readily undermine the legislative intent.

In appropriate circumstances, it should be foregone in favor of using the standard rules of interpretation, taking into account the statutory provision's wording, content, and policy to establish whose acts (knowledge or state of mind) was to be considered the company's acts or state of mind.

4.8.4. Criticism of the Identification Doctrine

According to some prosecutors, academics, and practicing attorneys, the Tesco v. Nattrass standard is insufficient for holding businesses accountable for criminal activity. Critics claim that to escape accountability, it encourages businesses to decentralize responsibility, making it challenging to pinpoint a senior person in control of a certain activity.

The Tesco v Nattrass test prevents commercial organizations from being held criminally liable in circumstances where there has been a collective failure at board level, but it is not possible to attribute particular failings to specific individuals.

When looking into small businesses, prosecutors typically have no trouble demonstrating that someone in a senior position in the management hierarchy had the necessary intent to commit the crime. However, it is believed that this regulation makes it impossible for a huge modern multinational firm to be successfully prosecuted because many businesses will have complicated management systems. These have the effect of insulating those identified as the directing mind and will of the company, as defined in Tesco v Nattrass, from allegations of knowledge of or complicity in the crime.

4.9. THE PROBLEM OF "ECONOMIC CRIME"

4.9.1. Growth in International and National Scale

Criminal conduct involving businesses, whether it be in the form of money-laundering, fraud, bribery, or tax evasion, seems to be becoming less amenable to standard legal tactics and has reached a size with serious economic ramifications. In the aftermath of the global financial crisis (GFC), evidence of misconduct is emerging that has never before "occurred so systematically, in such a scale and across multiple jurisdictions" (Figure 4.3).

Figure 4.3. Criminal activity involving companies in terms of money-laundering, fraud, bribery, or tax evasion.

Source: Image by Martin Kenny.

The estimates globally for money-laundering are truly eye-watering. According to research conducted by the UN Office on Drugs and Crime the amounts available for money laundering in 2009 were equivalent to 3.6% of GDP or US$ 2.1 trillion with money flows relating to transnational organized crime activities equivalent to 1.5% of global GDP or US$ 870 billion.

Furthermore, 70% of these money flows would have been available for laundering through the financial system, equivalent to 1% of global GDP or US$ 590 billion. The UK's National Crime Agency believes that "many hundreds of billions of international criminal money are laundered through UK banks, including their subsidiaries, each year."

Money laundering is viewed by HM Treasury and the Home Office as a major enabler of serious and organized crime, posing a threat to national security and incurring costs to society and the economy that are estimated to be £24 billion annually.

Reflecting perhaps the increasing priority attached to this issue, the FCA announced its largest penalty ever for a failure to maintain an adequate anti-money laundering (AML) control framework against Deutsche Bank AG, being a fine of just over £163 million in January 2017.

There is some debate over the estimates of the cost and volume of bribery, which may be different. Estimates indicate that the scale of the problem internationally has grown from $1.1 trillion in 2005 to between $1.5 trillion to $2 trillion in 2015.

The proportion of companies that must pay bribes to win or retain business varies enormously globally, 15% in industrialized countries, 30% in Asia and 60% in former Soviet Union countries.

The position in the UK is unclear; however, some idea of the potential scale of the problem may be shown by the record payment of £497.25 million plus interest and costs by Rolls-Royce plc under the terms of a Deferred Prosecution Agreement made with the Serious Fraud Office (SFO) in 2017, following a four-year investigation into bribery and corruption, with the total paid out by Rolls-Royce being approximately £671 million when payments to the US and Brazil were taken into account.

The Ministry of Justice has noted that the costs of bribery are frequently indirect or hidden and may include: contracts that are not properly specified or enforced, such as services that are not provided to the required standard or that are over specified with unnecessary gold plating; transaction costs that may be higher; competition that is hampered; incentives to invest and innovate that are undermined; serious reputational damage and strategic disruption if concerns arise.

However, in the case of bribery, it has been argued that the innovative approach to imposing criminal liability in the Bribery Act 2010 has had a significant impact in addressing and perhaps reducing bribery in the UK.

Equally eye-watering are the global estimates for fraud. PKF have estimated that in 2013 the global loss from fraud might have cost an equivalent of £2.78 trillion, more than 50% greater than the UK's entire GDP for the period.

Losses were measured in a wide variety of categories, including those related to industry, such as agriculture, construction, education, and housing, as well as those related to activities, such as remuneration, payroll, and procurement.

Using the terminology employed in the National Fraud Indicator, fraud alone is estimated to have cost the UK economy a staggering £193 billion in 2016, rising from £52 billion in 2013. Even though fraud received a lot of legal attention in the Fraud Act 2006, it is still a problem that affects a lot of people. The exponential increase in the amount estimated throughout that time may be explained more by other variables than by a particularly rapid increase in fraudulent conduct.

Beyond the quantifiable monetary cost, there is also a documented social cost of economic crime, including small businesses put into bankruptcy, livelihoods destroyed, employment destroyed, and chances missed, as well as the incalculable influence on society and people's health and well-being.

Given that they acknowledge frauds committed against organizations but not necessarily those allegedly committed by them, it is even possible that the global figures for fraudulent behavior mentioned above drastically underestimate the true degree of fraudulent behavior.

This is not intended as criticism, but rather to illustrate the various techniques that may be used in the determination of what constitutes criminally fraudulent behavior. The authors have addressed this issue elsewhere in terms of how addressing off-balance sheet finance as a matter of accounting regulation means that its potential categorization as criminal fraud may be overlooked.

Addressing other types of wrongdoing as issues of financial services regulation may have a similar impact. Accordingly, the 2016 Annual Fraud Indicator provides a comprehensive account of a number of types of fraud but does not refer to the various mis-selling cases that have pervaded the financial services industry.

Many of the various mis-selling stories that have made headlines in recent years may be judged to be fraud if put to the test in criminal courts. On this basis, £54 billion might be added to the figures, representing the total in compensation paid out by the major retail banks and building societies in the UK in the 15 years since 2000 for mis-selling activities.

In addition, further claims, currently estimated to amount to £33 billion, may result from the Supreme Court decision in Plevin v Paragon (2014) relating to the non-disclosure of sales commissions paid on these policies.

Interest rate hedging plans, packaged accounts, interest-only mortgages, investments, and other insurance products are only a few examples of the numerous other mis-selling concerns. Recently, it has been proposed that the responsibility for misspelling pension annuities may end up being just as severe as the incident involving personal protection insurance.

4.9.2. Legal Problems of Attribution Hinder Criminal Prosecution

The common law's approach to attributing criminal liability to companies, employing the so-called "identification principle," has posed serious difficulties. The Latin proverb "Actus non-facitreum nisi mens sit rea," which roughly translates as "Whatever the deed a man may have done, it cannot make him criminally punishable unless his doing of it was actuated by a legally blameworthy attitude of mind," traditionally expresses the common law foundation of criminal liability.

Additionally, the state of mind in question is decided upon subjectively rather than in accordance with an objective code of conduct, which is another aspect of the criminal law's individualist ideal. It has been observed that criminal responsibility can be sought in the context of corporate activities reveals many options.

In the first instance, an individual employee may commit the substantive offense in question and attract individual liability, for example under s. 1 Fraud Act for fraudulent activity of a proscribed type or s. 1, 2, or 6 of the Bribery Act 2010 for an offense of bribery, being bribed or bribing a foreign public official.

Regardless of whether the misconduct was intended to benefit the company, the responsibility rests with the individual engaged, unless that person holds a position of authority inside the organization that makes him the controlling mind. The "identification doctrine" may apply in this situation, making the firm itself legally accountable for the substantive offense.

Application of this doctrine means that a corporation can be found guilty of a substantive offense, for example fraud contrary to s. 1 Fraud Act or one of the bribery offenses set out at as. 1, 2, and 6 Bribery Act, the mensrea, namely the dishonesty and/or relevant intent, of the senior individual being attributable to the corporate entity itself.

Additionally, if the firm is found to be responsible under this concept, other corporate officers may also be held accountable if they helped to commit the crime by giving their consent or providing assistance. Criminal responsibility is limited in terms of corporate accountability to situations when the person who is considered to be the "directing mind and will" of the corporation, acting on its behalf, is also accountable for the offense.

The construction of corporate liability on this basis is now dated in that it is premised in a notion of corporations comprising relatively simple, pyramidal managerial frameworks.

This indicates that smaller businesses, whose directors are more likely to be involved in the day-to-day operations of the business, are considerably more likely to be convicted than large corporations, which often have complicated organizational structures and decentralized responsibilities.

The "identification principle" has been criticized for underestimating the nuance and complexity of corporate activity by applying an already oversimplified biological model to a similarly oversimplified understanding of business management and behavior.

In reality, corporate policy and decision-making is frequently decentralized or the outcome of other corporate rules and procedures as opposed to the outcome of individual decisions. Indeed, the "identification principle" of liability attribution serves as a real incentive to senior managers to "turn a blind eye" to questionable or dubious practices and it acts as a disincentive for the internal reporting of suspected illegality.

Therefore, as a method of attributing criminal liability, "it fails to reflect the reality of the modern day large multinational corporation and it produces what many regard as an unsatisfactory narrow scope for criminal liability." Additionally, the need to establish the criminality of an individual with sufficient seniority as a prerequisite to corporate prosecution creates evidence issues, which invariably worsen as the firm grows.

4.10. CONCLUSION

The scope and likelihood of corporate criminal responsibility were highlighted in this chapter's discussion of LIBOR manipulation. A general overview of LIBOR, the LIBOR scandal, and an illustration of the LIBOR scandal were discussed at the beginning of the chapter.

This chapter's middle section discusses LIBOR improvements, unforeseen effects of the new LIBOR system, and corporate accountability in more detail. This chapter concludes with a discussion of common law principles and, finally, the issue of economic crime.

REFERENCES

1. *Corporate Criminal Liability a Discussion Paper* – Amazon Web Services, inc., (n.d.). Available at: https://s3-eu-west-2.amazonaws.com/lawcom-prod-storage-11jsxou24uy7q/uploads/2021/06/Corporate-Criminal-Liability-Discussion-Paper.pdf (accessed on 15 June 2023).
2. Fernando, J., (2023). *What was the Libor Scandal? What Happened and Impacted Companies*. Investopedia. Available at: https://www.investopedia.com/terms/l/libor-scandal.asp#toc-example-of-the-libor-scandal (accessed on 15 June 2023).
3. Ministry of Justice, (2020). *Corporate Liability for Economic Crime: Call for Evidence*. GOV.UK. Available at: https://www.gov.uk/government/consultations/corporate-liability-for-economic-crime-call-for-evidence (accessed on 15 June 2023).
4. *New Models of Corporate Criminality and the Problem of Corporate Fraud*, (n.d.). Available at: https://eprints.bournemouth.ac.uk/29850/1/Economic%20crime%20article%20final%20draft%206.6.17%20%281%29.pdf (accessed on 15 June 2023).
5. *OECD Convention on Combating Bribery of Foreign Public Officials in International Business Transactions,* (n.d.). *OECD*. Available at: https://www.oecd.org/corruption/OECDantibriberyconvention.htm (accessed on 15 June 2023).
6. *Seeing Through the LI(E)BOR: Reforming the Libor Reforms,* (n.d.). Available at: https://scholarcommons.sc.edu/cgi/viewcontent.cgi?article=1119&context=scjilb (accessed on 15 June 2023).

CHAPTER 5

Corruption, Money Laundering, and Societal Responsibility of Banks

Contents

This chapter talks about the Corruption, Money laundering and Social Responsibility of banks. At the beginning of the chapter, this chapter explains about the introduction of corruption and money laundering. The chapter also addresses the Anti money laundering, History of Anti money laundering and bank secrecy. The chapter provides the highlights on the Bank Secrecy Act (BSA), Banks, and Societal Responsibility and Importance of Corporate Responsibility in the Banking Sector.

5.1. INTRODUCTION

Globally speaking, corruption is a problem that both industrialized and developing nations must deal with. The method used to conduct corrupt transactions varies depending on the situation. The types and levels of corrupt transactions are likely to be influenced and driven by factors such as the business sector (e.g., the construction, extractive, and defense industries), business activity types (e.g., contracts for goods and services, obtaining licenses and permits), economic opportunities (or lack thereof), and the political environment.

To illustrate, Rolls Royce has been in the news recently for engaging in corrupt transactions in China, Indonesia, and India.

Another illustration is the corruption issue involving Wal-attempts Mart's to penetrate the Indian and Mexican retail markets. And this is only the tip of the iceberg. A number of other global corporations, like Siemens and BAE, have also engaged in corrupt behavior.

The investigations and prosecutions brought by the United States' Security Exchange Commission under the US Foreign Corrupt Practices Act 1977, for instance, provides ample evidence.

To produce a result that benefits all parties involved in a corrupt transaction, a variety of tactics, including bid rigging, the trading of influence, and bribery, are employed. Bribery is the most easily understood within this range and according to an oft-quoted World Bank study '[a] conservative approach gives an estimate for annual worldwide bribery of about USD 1 trillion dollars (USD 1,000 billion.).'

The illegal funds collected through bribery invariably end up in bank accounts and are frequently moved to banks in other countries. For instance, according to Global Witness two Nigerian state governors who had been accepting bribes had deposited millions of pounds in a number of well-known UK banks: Barclays, HSBC, and RBS.

In the 1990s, there was a public recognition of the issue of corruption and bribery as well as the negative relationship between corruption, economic development, and growth. As a result of the subsequent anti-corruption debate at the global level, anti-corruption conventions at the regional and global levels as well as codes of conduct aimed at the conduct of public and private institutions and individuals working within them were adopted.

As a result of the anti-corruption discourse linking anti-money laundering (AML) measures as a corruption prevention mechanism as well as the fact that a significant portion of the funds obtained through corruption and bribery are moved across jurisdictions using financial institutions, provisions focusing on money laundering have been incorporated into the anti-corruption mechanisms.

Focusing on the link between corruption and money laundering (i.e., 'a process that employs financial, accounting, legal, and other instruments in conjunction with an object that has either been used in, or derived from, unlawful activity') this chapter explores the extent to which the AML framework has the potential to prevent corruption.

Consequently, the chapter first examines the anti-corruption treaties, particularly the United Nations Convention against Corruption (UNCAC), and how they incorporate the AML rhetoric into their broader framework. It is followed with an examination of due diligence procedures including those in relation to PEPs (politically exposed persons) that banks are expected to follow to counter money laundering (Figure 5.1).

Figure 5.1. Corruption.

Source: Image by Flickr.

This chapter argues that AML legislative measures (be they hard or soft) are of limited use only since they depend on rigorous application by the banks. It bases this argument on the UK Financial Services Authority's (FSA) 2011 Report on the managing of money laundering risks by banks and the HSBC money laundering case.

This chapter makes the case that banks should not only be profit-seeking organizations but should also consider their societal responsibilities, both locally and globally, to improve the contribution of AML measures to combat corruption. Banks, which in some cases encourage this activity through their commitment to bank secrecy, should not only be profit-seeking organizations.

If banks approached PEPs and high-risk customers from this angle, the motivation to do so would be reduced, enhancing the battle against corruption.

And it is understood that adoption of such an approach on the banks' part would also curb other social ills such as human trafficking and drug trafficking that are the sources of illicit funds and terrorist activities that use illicitly or illegitimately obtained funds for the furtherance of their causes and ideologies.

5.2. CORRUPTION AND MONEY LAUNDERING – THE LINK

Before discussing how money laundering and corruption are related, it is crucial to briefly discuss the two categories of corruption that are frequently mentioned in anti-corruption discussions: petty corruption and grand corruption.

Petty corruption is typically understood to be the type of corruption that people in society and the private sector deal with on a daily basis when trying to access basic services like getting access to utilities, getting passports, enrolling their children in school, and dealing with customs procedures.

On the other hand, grand corruption is typically regarded to be corruption that occurs at the highest levels of society and involves the political elite, public officials, middlemen, and the private sector. For instance, bribes paid to the political elite in arms procurement are an illustration of grand corruption. Grand corruption normally involves millions of dollars in contrast to petty corruption. Furthermore, money laundering is most affected by this kind of corruption. It's likely that the dishonest officials will want to hide the sources of the illegally obtained monies, and they will employ a variety of techniques to make this possible.

The most important of them is the usage of banks in nations where bank confidentiality is upheld, such Switzerland and Lichtenstein. Money earned through corruption can be used to purchase other assets like mansions and yachts in addition to bank deposits. The launderer is eager to produce a veneer of cleanliness during the laundering procedure (Figure 5.2).

Figure 5.2. Money laundering concept.

Source: Image by Flickr.

As Hinterseer notes: 'This veil not only prevents the object's association with unlawful activity from being accurately traced and identified, but also enables the object to be used in the legal economy with anonymity and without fear of criminal, civil or equitable sanction.'

5.3. WHAT IS ANTI-MONEY LAUNDERING (AML)?

The network of laws, rules, and processes known as AML aims to identify attempts to pass off criminal payments as legitimate income. Small-time tax evasion, drug trafficking, public corruption, and the funding of organizations classified as terrorist organizations are all crimes that are intended to be covered up by money laundering (Figure 5.3).

Figure 5.3. Anti-money laundering enforcement.

Source: Image by Flickr.

The emergence of the financial sector, the abolition of global capital controls, and the rising simplicity of executing intricate webs of financial transactions all led to the creation of AML regulation.

A high-level United Nations panel has estimated annual money laundering flows at $1.6 trillion, accounting for 2.7% of global GDP in 2020.

The 1970 Bank Secrecy Act (BSA) mandated that banks report cash deposits of more than $10,000, but AML regulations in the US have since grown to include a complex regulatory framework requiring financial institutions to conduct due diligence on their clients and look for and report suspicious transactions.

Similar laws have been passed by the European Union and other nations. Compliance for banks begins with confirming the identification of new clients, a procedure frequently referred to as "know your customer" (KYC). Banks must know a customer's behavior and confirm deposited monies are from a valid source in addition to verifying the customer's identity.

The KYC process also requires banks and brokers to screen new customers against lists of crime suspects, individuals, and companies under economic sanctions, and "PEPs"—foreign public officials, their family members, and close associates.

Money laundering can be divided into three steps:

- Deposit of illicit funds into the financial system;

- Transactions designed to conceal the illicit origin of the funds, known as "layering;"
- Use of laundered funds to acquire real estate, financial instruments, or commercial investments.

The KYC process aims to stop such schemes at the first deposit window.

5.3.1. Customer Due Diligence

The KYC procedure is not complete without conducting customer due diligence, for instance by verifying the veracity and accuracy of the information a prospective customer gives. It also involves both old and new clients, as well as their transactions, and is a continuous activity.

Each client's potential for money laundering must be continuously assessed as part of customer due diligence, and those clients who are recognized as posing higher non-compliance risks must be subject to more thorough due diligence. Identifying clients is part of that process as they are included to sanctions and other AML lists.

According to the U.S. Treasury's financial crimes enforcement network (FinCEN), the four core requirements of customer due diligences in the U.S. are:

- Identifying and verifying the customer's identity;
- Identifying and verifying the identity of beneficial owners with a stake of 25% or more in a company opening an account;
- Understanding the nature and purpose of customer relationships to develop customer risk profiles;
- Conducting on-going monitoring to identify and report suspicious transactions and update customer information.

Layering and structuring, commonly referred to as "smurfing"—the splitting up of large money laundering transactions into smaller ones to circumvent reporting requirements and avoid scrutiny—are money laundering techniques that customer due diligence aims to catch.

The AML holding period, which mandates that deposits must stay in an account for at least five trading days before they can be transferred elsewhere, is one regulation in place to prevent layering.

Financial institutions must create and implement a documented AML compliance policy that is managed by a designated AML compliance officer and must have written approval from a senior management member. These programs must specify "risk-based procedures for conducting ongoing customer due diligence" and conduct "on-going monitoring to identify and report suspicious transactions."

5.4. HISTORY OF ANTI-MONEY LAUNDERING (AML)

Efforts to police illicit gains have a history stretching back centuries, while the term "money laundering" is only about 100 years old and in wide use for less than 50.

The first major piece of U.S. AML legislation was the 1970 BSA, passed in part to thwart organized crime. The law mandated that banks identify the parties involved in transactions and keep track of them in addition to forcing banks to report cash deposits of more than $10,000.

The U.S. Supreme Court upheld the BSA's constitutionality in 1974, the same year "money laundering" entered wide use amid the Watergate scandal.

Along with growing attempts to combat drug trafficking, additional legislation was introduced in the 1980s, 1990s, and 2000s to improve financial monitoring and stop funding for terrorist organizations.

In 1989, a collection of nations and international organizations established the financial action task force (FATF), which helped anti-money laundering gain more global attention. The organization's goal is to create and encourage the adoption of global standards to combat money laundering. In October 2001, following the 9/11 terrorist attacks, FATF expanded its mandate to include combating terrorist financing.

Another important organization in the fight against money laundering is the International Monetary Fund (IMF). In an effort to stop the financing of terrorism, the IMF, like the FATF, has pressured its member nations to adhere to international standards.

The United Nations included AML provisions in its 1998 Vienna Convention addressing drug trafficking, the 2001 Palermo Convention against international organized crime and the 2005 Merida Convention against corruption.

The most comprehensive update to American AML laws since the Patriot Act of 2001 was the Anti-Money Laundering Act of 2020, passed in early 2021. The Corporate Transparency Act, part of the 2021 legislation, makes it more difficult to utilize shell corporations to get around AML and economic sanctions regulations.

The law also required art and antiquities merchants and cryptocurrency exchanges to do consumer due diligence in accordance with the same standards as financial organizations (Figure 5.4).

Figure 5.4. Crypto currency.

Source: Image by PixaHive.

5.5. THE ANTI-MONEY LAUNDERING (AML) STANDARDS – THE FATF STANDARDS

The FATF is a crucial architect in the establishment of protocols for enhancing best practices by financial institutions to prevent money laundering. To account for new money laundering patterns and strategies, the 1996 amendments to the initial 40 recommendations adopted in 1990.

The initial focus of these recommendations was on money laundering associated with the drug trade, but their purview has since been broadened to also cover funding for terrorism and terrorist organizations. The special recommendations on terrorist financing were enacted in 2001 to take into account these modifications.

The Recommendations underwent further revisions in 2003 and 180 countries endorsed these Recommendations together with the Special Recommendations. They formed the international standard for AML and countering terrorist financing.

These 40 recommendations and the special recommendations were revised further after the third round of mutual evaluations undertaken by the FATF and the new FATF Recommendations (Recommendations) were adopted in February 2012. In drafting the Recommendations, the FATF worked also in close co-operation with FATF style regional bodies (FSRBs), thus ensuring global effect.

Members of the FATF and the FSRBs are expected to adopt the Recommendations, which are accompanied by Interpretive Notes and a Glossary (these make up the FATF Standards). As before, a strict mutual assessment system is in place to evaluate their application. The FATF also offers best practice chapters and guidelines to assist members in implementing the Standards as effectively as possible.

The FATF Standards require 'countries to criminalize money laundering on the basis of the Vienna Convention (United Nations Convention against Illicit Traffic in Narcotic Drugs and Psychotropic Substances, 1988) and the Palermo Convention (United Nations Convention against Transnational Organized Crime 2000)' and to 'apply the crime of money laundering to all serious offenses, with a view to including the widest range of predicate offenses' in its Recommendation.

Predicate offenses are to be defined by reference to all offenses, to a threshold associated with a category of significant offenses, to the consequence of imprisonment, to a list of predicate offenses, or to a combination of these approaches, according to the Interpretive Note to Recommendation. It is up to the nations to decide what works best for them.

Regardless of the strategy used, all offenses falling under the specified categories of offenses must be considered, according to the Interpretive. The General Glossary provides the definition of "a designated group of offenses," which expressly mentions corruption and bribery.

The list also includes other offenses such as piracy, extortion, counterfeiting, and tax crimes. For our purposes the FATF Standards clearly link corruption and bribery with money laundering and in that they converge with the UNCAC.

5.6. BANK SECRECY

The BSA, also known as the Currency and Foreign Transactions Reporting Act, is a piece of legislation that was adopted by the US Congress in 1970 that mandates cooperation between US financial institutions and the US government in cases of alleged fraud and money laundering. In addition to making, it more difficult for money laundering to spread, the BSA's goal is to stop banks from acting as unaware intermediaries for illegal conduct (Figure 5.5).

Figure 5.5. Foreign currency and coins.

Source: Image by Flickr.

The BSA mandates that banks report transactions involving more than $10,000 in cash from a single customer because of a single transaction or two or more connected transactions that take place within a 24-hour period in order to assist in the fight against money laundering.

Cash is described as any kind of money, including coins and bills from the United States and other nations as well as specific financial instruments such money orders, traveler's checks, cashier's checks, and bank drafts. Cash is not regarded as a personal check.

Banks are also required by the BSA to disclose any suspicious conduct that could be a sign of fraud or money laundering. A transaction is deemed suspicious if it contains $5,000 or more in monies or assets that the financial institution believes may be used to conceal illicit behavior or suggest profit from it.

The BSA mandates that a number of institutions, including casinos, firms that issue or redeem money orders, and dealers in precious metals and gemstones, in addition to conventional financial institutions like banks and brokers, report suspicious behavior.

AML laws and the BSA are sometimes used interchangeably. To date, a number of AML laws, including clauses in title III of the USA PATRIOT Act, have been passed to alter the BSA. The legislation is enforced by the FinCEN.

The request to maintain secrets has long been made of bankers, clergy, and medical professionals. Following World War 1, the regulations governing bank secrecy were created. The argument that banks secrecy exists to "protect people from financial loss in countries afflicted by instability, weak currency, and runaway inflation rates" is frequently used to defend it.

Bank secrecy is also thought to safeguard affluent people or those who support unpopular political ideologies by enabling them to conceal their assets and shield themselves from the risk of kidnapping or persecution.

Any discussion of bank secrecy has to start with the Swiss Banking Law 1934. Although bank secrecy in Switzerland had been evident from the 16th-century it was in 1934 that it was formally codified, and according to Article 47(b) of this Law anyone that breaches the secrecy rule attracts a sanction.

This clause safeguards and privileges the client-banker relationship, and it makes it illegal to disclose a person's financial information, except for situations in which that person has been charged with a crime.

The implication of this is that a customer's financial information cannot be disclosed, and more crucially, a third party's inquiry should not be answered. Furthermore, certain banks often employ numbered bank accounts, while others give pseudonyms. Both methods are designed to make tracing and disclosure more challenging.

The Swiss Banking Law, which is an illustration of the types of legal provision governing bank secrecy, is often said to have been initially developed for a benevolent purpose to prevent Nazi Germans attempting to investigate and seize assets, which were held in Switzerland by Jews.

Along with this assertion, Swiss bankers have asserted that bank secrecy is equivalent to a person's right to privacy. Europe has been especially sensitive to this need for privacy given its more recent history of totalitarian regimes. But not everyone agrees that this moral basis for Swiss financial secrecy is valid.

Several 100 tons of gold bullion were allegedly swapped from Hitler's central bank for Swiss francs in order to buy supplies like steel to help with the war effort. It has also been claimed that Swiss bank secrecy has throughout time led to Jewish people's bank accounts being confiscated by

Nazi Germans. And according to Faith the welfare justification myth has provided 'a flag of morality which they could wrap securely round them when they were accused of harboring criminals of every nationality and description.'

Although bank secrecy may have begun with 'good' intentions, it has been abused and perverted by organized crime and money laundering because of its very nature. Secrecy laws are also thought to be a way to attract foreign investment, which may be legitimate or criminal.

Although Swiss bankers have denied that money laundering is a problem, preferring to suggest tax evasion is the offense to be concerned about, there is no doubt that bank secrecy facilitates the laundering of illegal money.

There are currently six nations in Europe alone that have well-established bank secrecy arrangements, even though Switzerland is probably the most well-known example of a nation that advocates bank secrecy. To draw in foreign investment, bank secrecy has served as a valuable strategy throughout the world.

A requirement for this investment is bank secrecy, which is regarded as being vital in a number of Caribbean states for growth and prosperity. It has been suggested that these countries therefore find themselves 'stuck between a rock and a hard place.' According to others, maintaining bank secrecy is a necessary step towards advancing the economy.

Malkawi explains that some Arab countries have developed their bank secrecy arrangements in order to protect money launderers as a way of generating economic prosperity. These arrangements are said to 'embody national economic objectives.' In 2011 it was estimated that $7.8 trillion was currently being held offshore which goes some way to explain the magnitude of the problem globally.

Why are those who oppose bank secrecy rules so adamant that it is morally acceptable or a means of legitimate economic development? It would seem entirely reasonable for our personal financial transaction data to be kept private.

However, bank secrecy opponents are worried that because the system is secretive, it is impossible to determine where the money comes from.

Uncertainty about the source breeds suspicion, whether it is justified or not. In recent years, the literature has concentrated on the connection between bank secrecy and the laundering of money, which either the product of illegal activities like drug is trafficking and corruption or is used to support terrorism (including maritime piracy). The US has long been suspicious of bank secrecy. Prior to the passing of the BSA 1970 the House of Representatives Report commented:

'Secret foreign bank accounts and secret foreign financial institutions have permitted proliferation of "white collar" crime; have served as the financial underpinning of organized criminal operations in the United States; have been utilized by Americans to evade income taxes, conceal assets illegally and purchase gold...have served as essential ingredients in fraud including schemes to defraud the United States.'

In order to expedite both criminal and tax investigations, the BSA 1970 itself granted access to bank records of specific persons to government agencies. All significant overseas transactions had to be recorded, and banks had to disclose all relevant information regarding each customer's financial arrangements.

The Right to Financial Privacy Act 1978 (RFPA, 1978) provided safeguards for the sweeping powers of the BSA 1970 by requiring a search warrant to be obtained before an individual's records could be accessed.

These security measures are still simple to get through and notoriously tough to enforce. Because of Switzerland's tradition of bank secrecy, the US and Switzerland were able to establish a Memorandum of Understanding on Insider Trading in 1982.

Money laundering was deemed a crime in the United States in 1984, and the Money Laundering Control Act of 1988 made it unlawful to omit filing currency transaction reports. On account of its enforcement agenda taking precedence above any specific bank privacy concerns, the US legislative response to bank secrecy has been referred to as a "attack."

Following the 9/11 terrorist attacks the US passed Title III of the Patriot Act (The International Money Laundering Abatement and Anti-Terrorist Financing Act, 2011) which further strengthened the legal framework for combating money laundering and amended both the BSA1970 and the Money Laundering Act 1986 (MLA, 1986) by attempting to make it more difficult for money launderers to operate.

The Patriot Act compels banks to create and implement AML compliance programs, implement customer identification verification processes, forbids banks from keeping correspondent accounts for shell banks, and mandates greater due diligence for specific overseas accounts. Finally, this Act mandates that banks keep track of their clients' identification documents and disclose this data in response to any requests from law authorities. This reflects the FATF Standards.

The excessively onerous administrative burden placed on banks by the Patriot Act has drawn criticism. It is frequently argued that US banks may not be able to compete globally with other nations that have stricter rules governing bank secrecy. Panko rejects these criticisms and also focuses on what he refers to as the 'moderate, justifiable intrusions on customer privacy.'

The shortcomings of the pre-Patriot Act restrictions, according to Panko, allowed for the growth of terrorism. He focuses on the dangers of insufficient information exchange and mentions how the 9/11 hijackers were able to move their money into and around the US. Dismissing bank secrecy and privacy as being of secondary importance to transparency, Panko suggests critics fail to 'recognize the symbiotic relationship between bank secrecy and terrorist financing.' The US has since passed the Foreign Account Tax Compliance Act 2013 (FATCA), which is said to relieve some of the aforementioned administrative burdens (Figure 5.6).

Figure 5.6. Signing of the FATCA agreement.

Source: Image by Flickr.

The FATCA establishes important due diligence procedures, such as a requirement to report accounts owned by US citizens on an annual basis. Early indications indicate that non-compliant account holders "can no longer trust that they would remain undiscovered or protected by international banking secrecy regulations," albeit the full impact of this legislation has not yet been determined. The prevalence of money laundering and tax evasion because of bank secrecy regulations has been brought to light in two recent incidents, which have done so once again. The details of these episodes read like a thriller. The first of these scandals was the Liechtenstein Tax Affair. LGT is the primary financial institution in Liechtenstein.

The country's royal family owns it. It is currently estimated that £130 billion of foreigners' money is held in the country. A small very wealthy country where 'trust and secrecy are perhaps more valuable than money.'

In light of this, a data archivist by the name of Heinrich Kieber stole and sold a CD containing a list of clients who were tax evaders in their own nations. Kieber worked at LGT Treuhand a subsidiary of LGT, and he disclosed the names of around 1,250 out of 77,000 clients at LGT.

After making copies of the disc, he first tried to sell the data to the UK's Inland Revenue, but they originally turned him down. Kieber was able to make a $5.5 million sale of the material to the German Secret Service.

Since Kieber is wanted by Liechtenstein for violating Article 14 of the Liechtenstein Banking Act by disclosing sensitive information, it is currently believed that he is hiding out in Australia using a false identity. He is also wanted by Interpol for theft and fraud.

This scandal had a huge impact. Tax evasion had cost Germany a significant amount of money over the years, and Liechtenstein was no longer seen as a "safe bet" for offshore savings. Significant sums were also retrieved by other nations.

The UK was successful in recovering $4.75 billion in unpaid taxes, despite not having purchased the fraudulent CD but having agreed to partial disclosure of said accounts with Liechtenstein. From the data gathered, the US was able to show that US residents had been using LGT to evade taxes.

Due to the US's ignorance of the tax evaders, no prosecutions could be brought up until this point. They were able to ask LGT for more information after they received the bare bones of his bio. LGT refused, claiming a breach of the bank secrecy laws in Liechtenstein.

The US subsequently investigated LGT and its methods and learned that LGT had encouraged US citizens to register accounts with Liechtenstein foundations, acting as a shield for the US clients and shielding any assets from taxation.

Berger further points out that LGT set up the accounts in a way that got around the Qualified Intermediary rules, which call for the disclosure of specific accounts. Not only did these deeds show that US people were engaging in criminal behavior, but that LGT was also actively participating in it.

The Liechtenstein government harshly denounced Kieber's activities in the wake of this controversy, but it didn't appear to denounce LGT's, underscoring the significance of the country's bank secrecy regulations.

Instead, of calling for a relaxation of their bank secrecy restrictions, the response seems to have called for tightening them. Fascinatingly, some people view Kieber's behavior as an example of whistleblowing, and as a result, they view him as a hero rather than a criminal, even though the Liechtenstein government continues to call him a thief.

A comparable whistleblowing controversy occurred in 2007, but this time it included UBS in Switzerland. US nationals have previously opened accounts in Switzerland with UBS and LGT. Former UBS private banker and whistleblower Bradley Birkenfield. Birkenfield provided the US with documentation that concerned tax evasion by US clients.

The documentation included the details of US clients of the bank. There were 19,000 undisclosed accounts. This amounted to around $18 billion in lost revenue, which generated some $200 million profit for UBS.

Similar strategies were employed by UBS and LGT to conceal client bank information from the US Internal Revenue Service (IRS). Investigations revealed that UBS intentionally chose US clients because they are among the world's wealthiest investors. In the process of the investigations, it emerged that Birkenfield had actively worked with a US client, Igor Olenicoff, and had abated Olenicoff's extensive tax evasion.

Birkenfield was arrested and he pleaded guilty to tax evasion. Birkenfield was sentenced to 40 months imprisonment. At the same time, the US Department of Justice (DOJ) reached a deferred prosecution agreement with UBS and UBS paid a fine of $780 million.

UBS consented to divulge all information about their US clients, and the US clients were urged to participate in a Voluntary Disclosure Program (a type of amnesty program), which led to the recovery of overdue taxes of $2.7 billion. Birkenfield was successful in getting a $104 million prize after leaving prison.

Berger claims that there have been "far-reaching implications" from the LGT and UBS scandals. The visible indicting of bank workers has changed significantly, to start. Birkenfield and Raoul Weil, the head of UBS' Wealth

Management division, were both accused of conspiring to evade paying income taxes to the US. Martin Lack, a former head of UBS' North American business was also charged with conspiracy to defraud the US.

The goal of these high-profile arrests appears to be to obtain additional information about US clients hiding assets in Swiss bank accounts as well as to make a symbolic signal that individuals who provide this type of financial advice will face legal consequences. Birkenfield himself compared the Swiss banking industry with gangsters when he stated:

'In essence, bank secrecy is analogous to criminal racketeering- and the Swiss government, along with every Swiss private banker, is a co-conspirator.'

The comparison with the federal charges against Al Capone in 1931 for tax evasion is clear. The LGT and UBS scandals have also led to increasing efforts to promote better transparency. Crawford has verified that the secret bank has received more attention as a result of the current economic downturn. There has been some change in this environment.

To tax the money held by British nationals, Switzerland, and Great Britain have negotiated an agreement. Liechtenstein has also promised to relax its banking restrictions. The G20 nations took a more specific measure in 2009 by requiring those nations with bank secrecy rules to establish bilateral agreements that allow for the interchange of banking data.

The impact of this rule has been inconsistent. On the one hand, the OECD has said that these accords do greatly increase the possibility of identifying widespread tax evasion, which will inevitably boost tax collection.

The G20 plan still allows for bank secrecy, according to critics, and it appears that even while most tax evaders did not respond to the treaties, those who did ended up moving their savings to tax havens that were not covered by the treaty.

Additionally, the harmful effects of bank secrecy on the fight against corruption are highlighted in worldwide anti-corruption debate. For instance, the UNCAC in Article 40 provides that 'Each State Party shall ensure that, in the case of domestic criminal investigations of offenses established in accordance with this Convention, there are appropriate mechanisms available within its domestic legal system to overcome obstacles that may arise out of the application of bank secrecy laws.'

In 2009 world leaders at the G20 summit announced, 'the era of bank secrecy is over.' Five years on, the evidence suggests that although some progress has been made the era of bank secrecy continues. In order to break the relationship between corruption, money laundering, and bank secrecy, it appears from the debate of both the AML standards and the bank secrecy law that there is still a lot of ground to cover. It's crucial to stop right here and consider the function of banks.

Without a doubt, banks play a crucial role in the economy by safeguarding depositor money and providing vital funding for a variety of projects, whether they are commercial or private. Normal expectations are that banks will only engage in low-risk business initiatives and behave ethically, however as a result of increased rivalry brought on by globalization, banks have begun to engage in high-risk business endeavors in an effort to please their shareholders.

The ethical standards that the public may have held of banks appear to have been surpassed by profit. Major public opinion about banks has changed significantly because of the current financial crisis and the enormous bonuses awarded to bankers.

The validity and reputation of financial banks have consequently been impacted. This is made worse by the fact that reports from organizations like the FSA and Global Witness suggest that banks are collaborating with very corrupt PEPs to the disadvantage of the public in the corrupt countries.

Against this context how can these financial institutions rebuild their reputation and act in a manner that is motivated by ethics and not profit? The answer lies, we believe, in a philosophical shift that places societal responsibility at its core.

5.7. HOW THE BANK SECRECY ACT (BSA) WORKS?

The law does not require every transaction exceeding $10,000 to be documented. According to the IRS, there is a general rule that any person in a trade or business must file Form 8300 if their business receives more than $10,000 in cash from one buyer.

This can be the result of a single transaction or of two or more related transactions. The rule can apply to an individual; a company, corporation, partnership, association, or trust; or an estate.

By the 15th day following the cash transaction, Form 8300 must be submitted. If any portion of the monetary transactions takes place within the United States, its possessions, or its territories, then this requirement is applicable.

The law maintains a list of exclusions that do not require this level of investigation. Examples of excluded parties include government departments or agencies, as well as businesses listed on significant North American exchanges.

Although the BSA can be helpful in preventing crime, it has come under fire since so few rules specify what constitutes suspicious behavior. Law enforcement organizations can access the information without a court order as well.

The Office of the Comptroller of the Currency (OCC) regularly examines banks, federal savings associations, and other institutions for compliance with the BSA.

5.7.1. Criticism of the Bank Secrecy Act (BSA)

Financial institutions and law enforcement agencies all around the country are struggling under the weight of the BSA's massive volume of data collection, production, and maintenance requirements. Many anti-money-laundering professionals have questioned whether the government can successfully identify the "needle in the haystack" while looking into shady financial dealings.

The BSA was allegedly created in the era before the first laptop computer was made, so it has to be revised. Financial organizations struggle constantly with the rapidly evolving technologies for payments and transactions. The evolution of banking technology in the 21st century would be addressed by updates to tools to combat illicit activity.

5.7.2. Effects of the Bank Secrecy Act (BSA)

FinCEN, recognizes agencies that have used BSA data to successfully track and prosecute criminal inquiries.

The BSA serves a useful purpose by shielding the general public from hazards like fraud, cybercrime, and other unlawful financial activities that the US is subject to. The BSA and law enforcement have focused heavily on reducing criminality and taking advantage of those who are exposed to these schemes.

5.8. BANKS AND SOCIETAL RESPONSIBILITY

Before looking at the bank's role in societal responsibility it would make sense to say a few words on what societal responsibility encompasses.

We understand societal responsibility to include the duty of an individual and other entities (widely construed to include an institution, charitable establishment, company) to engage in a manner that engages with and takes into account the consequences of their intended actions and how these could affect the world at large.

It should be interpreted broadly to cover all factors that are harmful to the human condition rather than being narrowly focused on or limited to specific issues like the environment, working conditions, or child labor.

It is important to clarify this definition of societal duty from the frequently discussed concept of corporate social responsibility (CSR). Since there isn't agreement on what CSR genuinely implies, we make this distinction.

The responsibility of businesses vs that of the government was a topic of dispute that was prevalent in the 1950s. In the 1990s, the definition of CSR was expanded to encompass concerns for the environment, labor rights, workplace health and safety, and gender issues.

There is a great quantity of literature that covers anything from understanding CSR as responsible decision-making and practice, being responsive to include the interests of all stakeholders, to just reacting to external expectations and pressures.

International organizations like the UN, OECD, and World Bank have also joined the CSR conversation. Given the various ways that CSR might be interpreted, the most widespread agreement that can be reached is that, when a company produces substantial profits, its CSR obligations should go beyond philanthropic donations to the community.

As Carroll & Buchholtz note: 'What is particularly paradoxical is that large numbers of businesspeople have enthusiastically embraced the concept of CSR during the past three decades, but only limited consensus has emerged about what CSR really means.' It is common practice for banks to have CSR policies.

HSBC, a bank we referred to, earlier in the chapter does have a CSR policy. The emphasis on the environment and employment prospects, which are frequently mentioned in CSR reports from other business organizations, appears to be the main focus of its Sustainability Report, according to a reading of it.

The HSBC Report does talk about 'doing the right thing' as a result of the penalties that HSBC had to pay in the US and the resulting hit on their reputation.

However, acting morally appears to be more about reputation risk, or rebuilding their (the bank's) reputation (which is inextricably linked to revenues), than about society responsibility. Even though US regulatory authorities have looked into the affairs of the banks in great detail, this is still quite disappointing.

5.9. CORPORATE SOCIAL RESPONSIBILITY (CSR) IN THE BANKING SECTOR

The recent years have brought a significant increase in the interest in CSR and performance (CSP) on the part of all major stakeholder groups, including, in particular, equity investors, managers, and regulators (Figure 5.7).

Figure 5.7. Banking.

Source: Image by the Blue Diamond Gallery.

While CSP focuses on real results achieved in the field of social responsibility, CSR expands a company's social obligation beyond the interests of its owners to include employees, consumers, the government, community, and the environment.

CSR encompasses a wide range of proactive and reactive activities focused on both internal and external factors aimed at enhancing the economic, social, and environmental performance of enterprises, with respect to stakeholder expectations. The aforementioned elements, which include human moral obligations as well as external legal and market forces, have gradually evolved to play a significant role in determining how modern corporations behave. Banks should naturally be inclined to follow the road of social responsibility and engage in CSR-related activities even more frequently and profoundly than other businesses as their continued existence and viability are virtually totally dependent on the public's faith in them.

In addition to being more susceptible to reputational risk than other industries, banks are also more open to stakeholder and customer criticism. Not surprisingly, therefore, they are highly sensitive to environmental, social, and governance (ESG) risk, as it may directly affect both their financial performance and an overall operational risk exposure.

5.10. IMPORTANCE OF CORPORATE SOCIAL RESPONSIBILITY (CSR) IN THE BANKING SECTOR

The magnitude of banks' social impact is unquestionably significant given their position as major financial intermediaries and their global interconnectivity. Through involvement in the processes of capital accumulation and allocation as well as the effects of the banking sector's financial soundness and stability on the entire economy, the outcomes of their activities have an impact on society as a whole in addition to the well-being of their owners, employees, and clients.

Social responsibility of banks involves both the responsibility of individual institutions for the security of funds entrusted to them and the responsibility of the entire banking sector for the stability of the financial system and the economy.

A complex network of generally long-lasting interactions between banks and their external stakeholders also emerges as a result of the long-term nature of many bank goods and services. Therefore, the objectives of a bank's operations should not be limited to maximizing the profits of its owners but should also take into account the demands of other stakeholders and society at large.

Given the aforementioned, banks should be more encouraged to consider social responsibility when making commercial decisions and to share information on the scope and real results of the activities performed. Engagement in socially responsible activities offers banks additional opportunities to distinguish themselves from competitors and to improve the perceived quality of their services in the eyes of the public.

As pointed out by Ziolo, banks generally respond to the challenges of social responsibility with a certain delay in comparison with the real sphere. In reality, in the wake of the global financial crisis (GFC), which was primarily brought on by banks acting irresponsibly by heavily utilizing moral hazard to further their commercial objectives, the social performance of the banking industry garnered a unique amount of attention.

The record-high fines imposed by the regulators for the revealed misconduct forced the banking industry to restore the public's trust and to develop new, more transparent business models, incorporating social responsibility as an integral component of their strategies.

Despite significant progress, the financial services sector continues to be the least trusted industry despite the fact that the GFC began more than 10 years ago, according to the results of the most current 2021 Edelman Trust Barometer study.

On average only 52% of more than 33,000 respondents from 28 countries declared trust in it, which is 7% points less than the second worst-trusted entertainment sector, and 16% points less than the leading technology sector.

It is also important to note that the soundness of a bank's financial position is frequently a determining factor in how successfully it implements sustainability and social responsibility concepts into its business models due to the high explicit and implicit expenses involved.

In fact, there is strong feedback between banks' financial position and their social performance. On the one hand, the foundational elements of the CSR framework – such as adherence to moral and sustainable norms, openness in the conduct of business, and accuracy of financial disclosures – depend on long-term profitability to guarantee banks' health financially.

However, perceptions of a bank's business activities' perceived responsibility and ethics, as well as its financial status, have a significant impact on the public's trust in banks, their reputation, and their long-term viability.

These bidirectional connections expose banks to several CSR-related opportunities and risks. Despite the foregoing, research from transition economies indicates that even banks with decreased profitability can show significant commitment in socially responsible activities.

One of the key areas of CSR regards the quality and transparency of the disclosed information.

In general, the public, and in particular equity investors, demand socially conscious businesses to offer the most thorough and trustworthy data. In the case of banks, whose business strategies are typically very complex and opaque, this issue looks to be especially significant. Improved access to trustworthy and value-relevant information could help to reduce necessary risk premia and decrease investors' confusion about the anticipated economic performance of socially responsible banks. This, in turn, ceteris paribus, would lead to increases in the perceived market values of such banks.

The inherent worth of responsible banks should also be more precisely estimated by stock market analysts and knowledgeable equity investors, increasing the overall effectiveness of the capital market in that sector. According to this viewpoint, adhering to CSR principles may become a crucial component of listed banks' business strategy aimed at a sustained increase in their market values.

5.11. CONCLUSION

This chapter provided an overview of the topics of corruption, money laundering, and banks' civic responsibilities. The first section of this chapter explored corruption and money laundering, as well as what AML is and its history.

At the middle, this chapter explained about the AML standards, bank secrecy and how the BSA works.

Towards the end of the chapter, chapter elaborate about banks and societal responsibility, CSR in the banking sector and at last but not the least importance of CSR in the banking sector.

REFERENCES

1. Carr, I. M., & Jago, R., (2014). *Corruption, Money Laundering, Secrecy, and Societal Responsibility of Banks*. researchgate.net. Available at: https://www.researchgate.net/publication/272300127_Corruption_Money_Laundering_Secrecy_and_Societal_Responsibility_of_Banks (accessed on 15 June 2023).
2. Carr, I. M., & Jago, R., (2014). *Corruption, Money Laundering, Secrecy, and Societal Responsibility of Banks*. SSRN. Available at: https://papers.ssrn.com/sol3/papers.cfm?abstract_id=2454934 (accessed on 15 June 2023).
3. Carr, I., & Jago, R., (2014). *Corruption, Money Laundering and Societal Responsibility of Banks*. Royal Holloway Research Portal. Routledge. Available at: https://pure.royalholloway.ac.uk/en/publications/corruption-money-laundering-and-societal-responsibility-of-banks (accessed on 15 June 2023).
4. Carr, I., & Jago, R., (n.d.). *Corruption, Money Laundering, Secrecy, and Societal Responsibility of Banks*. edisciplinas. Available at: https://edisciplinas.usp.br/pluginfile.php/4282100/mod_resource/content/0/CORRUPTION%2C%20MONEY%20LAUNDERING%2C%20SECRECY%20AND%20SOCIETAL%20RESPONSIBILITY%20OF%20BANKS.pdf (accessed on 15 June 2023).
5. *Corporate Social Responsibility in the Banking Sector*, (n.d.). Encyclopedia. Available at: https://encyclopedia.pub/entry/16083#:~:text=Social%20responsibility%20of%20banks%20involves,financial%20system%20and%20the%20economy (accessed on 15 June 2023).
6. Fundanga, C. M., (n.d.). *The Role of the Banking Sector in Combating Money Laundering*. www.bis.org. The C and N Centre for Advanced International Studies. Available at: https://www.bis.org/review/r030212f.pdf (accessed on 15 June 2023).
7. Kenton, W., (2022). *Bank Secrecy Act (BSA): Definition, Purpose, and Effects*. Investopedia. Available at: https://www.investopedia.com/terms/b/bank_secrecy_act.asp#toc-effects-of-the-bank-secrecy-act (accessed on 15 June 2023).
8. Kenton, W., (2023). *Anti Money Laundering (AML) Definition: Its History and How it Works*. Investopedia. Available at: https://www.investopedia.com/terms/a/aml.asp (accessed on 15 June 2023).

9. *What is Bank Secrecy Act (BSA)? Definition,* (2009). WhatIs.com. TechTarget. Available at: https://www.techtarget.com/whatis/definition/Bank-Secrecy-Act-BSA (accessed on 15 June 2023).

CHAPTER 6

The Good, the Bad and the Fraud: Securitization and Financial Crime in Light of the Global Financial Crisis

Contents

This chapter discusses the Securitization and Financial crime in light of the global financial crisis (GFC). At the beginning of this chapter, the chapter explains about the introduction and history of securitization. This chapter also addresses the parties involved in securitization and types of securitized instruments. The end of the chapter provides highlights on the Benefits of Securitization, The allure of Securitizing and Advantages of Securitization.

6.1. INTRODUCTION TO SECURITIZATION

The process of pooling assets to repackage them into interest-bearing securities is known as securitization. The underlying assets' principal and interest payments are given to the investors who buy the repackaged securities.

When an issuer creates a marketable financial instrument by combining or pooling different financial assets, such as several mortgages, the securitization process gets started. The issuer then offers investors this collection of repackaged assets. Securitization provides investors with opportunities and releases funds for originators, both of which encourage market liquidity.

In theory, any financial asset can be securitized—that is, turned into a tradeable, fungible item of monetary value. In essence, this is what all securities are.

Most of the time, however, securitization involves loans and other assets that produce receivables, such as various forms of consumer or commercial debt. It might entail combining contractual commitments like auto loans and credit card debts.

The decades-old idea of securitization has received a bad rap because of the subprime mortgage crisis that started in 2007. In the process of securitization, specific asset classes are gathered together in order to be repackaged into interest-bearing securities. The holders of the securities are given a pass-through of the interest and principal payments from the assets.

When home mortgages were bundled by institutions backed by the US government in the 1970s, securitization first emerged. Other income-producing assets first started to be securitized in the 1980s, and the industry has expanded significantly in recent years.

Investor confidence was weakened in several markets due to the unanticipated decline in the quality of some of the underlying assets, such as those for securities backed by hazardous subprime mortgages in the

United States. Both the scale and persistence of the attendant credit crisis seem to suggest that securitization—together with poor credit origination, inadequate valuation methods, and insufficient regulatory oversight—could severely hurt financial stability.

Securitization is a strategy used by an increasing number of financial institutions to offload the credit risk associated with the assets they originate from their balance sheets and onto the books of other financial institutions, including banks, insurance companies, and hedge funds. There are several reasons why they do it.

It is often cheaper to raise money through securitization, and securitized assets were then less costly for banks to hold because financial regulators had different standards for them than for the assets that underpinned them. The "originate and distribute" strategy, which spread out credit risks and reduced systemic vulnerabilities, theoretically also had significant economic advantages.

Until the subprime crisis unfolded, the impact of securitization was largely positive and benign. However, some have accused securitization of undermining originators' incentives to uphold the bare minimum of prudent lending, risk management, and investment standards at a time when investors were being enticed to take on more risk due to low returns on conventional debt products, default rates below historical norms, and the accessibility of numerous hedging tools.

The fact that many of the loans were not held on the balance sheets of those who securitized them may have encouraged originators to reduce the amount of time they spent vetting and monitoring potential borrowers, which may have contributed to a general decline in lending and collateral standards.

6.2. HISTORY OF SECURITIZATION

6.2.1. Early History

Under Roman law, people had the ability to issue long-term debt and secure it with land. Long-term debts are issued using two different methods: pignus and hypothec. Property that serves as security for a loan is transferred to the lender in a pignus and will be returned upon loan repayment. The property was still the borrowers in hypothec, but the lender might confiscate it if the borrower fell behind on the payments.

By the 11th and 12th century, mortgages were used to finance Crusades. Baldwin of Ghent is said to have financed his participation in the First Crusade by mortgaging his Curtis of Ootegan to a local abbey for 42 marks. Godfrey III, Duke of Brabant mortgaged his fief of Herstal to the Bishop of Liège for 300 marks to finance his journey to Jerusalem in 1171.

Landowners in Northern France employed a method known as bail à rente (rent sale) in the 12th-century to transfer the obligation to pay land rent to a third party in exchange for a capital sum. A written commitment to pay a stated annuity, in produce or in money, out of the income of a certain property, bail à rente is an evolution of the feudal practice of putting a rent-charge on land.

The property used to secure the annuity was easier for the creditor to seize in the event of default because this was viewed as a sale as opposed to a loan. In the 18th-century when British set fire to Copenhagen, a similar mechanism to modern day securitization was used to lend money to borrowers to build new buildings.

In Copenhagen in 1850, the first Mortgage Credit Act is published. Modern securitization is thought to have originated in Denmark.

Figure 6.1. Pfandbrief Süddeutsche Bodencreditbank.

Source: Image by Wikimedia Commons.

The Pfandbrief, a conventional mortgage financing method developed in Germany, is still used today. The conventional mortgage trading instrument with a 200-year history in Germany is known as a pfandbrief. Asset-backed bonds are Pfandbrief. Unlike contemporary asset-backed bonds, the underlying asset is still present on the issuer's balance sheet. Pfandbrief institution acts as a massive SPV (Figure 6.1).

The German Federal Banking Supervisor appoints a trustee, who monitors the sufficiency of the collaterals to cover required payments on a regular basis. To sell underlying assets, the bank in charge of the pool must obtain the trustee's consent.

In the event of a default by the issuer, the bondholders have access to the underlying assets. Pfandbrief holders rank as the top creditors in the event of the issuer's liquidation if the underlying assets are adequate to pay all outstanding payments to them. By 2005, the total value of pfandbrief issue amounted to 137.9 Euro.

6.2.2. US Mortgage Market

During the Great Depression, the deposit market experienced a major collapse. In order to establish a secondary market for mortgages, the National Housing Act was passed into law. In 1934, the Federal Housing Administration (FHA) was created.

FHA was to insure housing loans granted by private lenders, which will absorb the risk of default. In 1938, Federal National Mortgage Association (FNMA) was created with the idea of buying and selling federally insured mortgages. In 1968, FNMA was divided into two namely, FNMA, and Government National Mortgage Association (GNMA).

Modern improvements in the securitization business were facilitated by FNMA and GNMA. The FNMA first issued a security backed by a mortgage in 1981. It had been extremely important in pushing the securitization of adjustable and variable rate mortgages.

The first attempts to securitize financial assets were made in the past, as mentioned above, in the US mortgage lending markets. The US government took action to create companies that acquire and sell mortgages. The purpose was to establish a secondary market for mortgage lending. In the US government sponsored entities (GSEs) (Freddie Mac, Ginnie Mae, and Fannie Mae) contributed to making a secondary market in mortgages. Literature therefore indicates that the founding of Freddie Mac by the US government in 1970 marked the start of the modern age of securitization. In the cases of Fannie Mae, Freddie Mac, and Ginnie Mae, the US government was impliedly (in the case of Freddie Mac) and officially (in the case of Ginnie Mae) "backed" by the securities issued by these GSEs, giving investors assurance that their investments would be fully and promptly paid for (Figure 6.2).

Figure 6.2. Federal National Mortgage Association, or "Fannie Mae," headquarters building in Washington, D.C.

Source: Image by Picryl.

6.3. PARTIES INVOLVED IN SECURITIZATION

The main parties involved in the process of securitization are discussed in subsections.

6.3.1. Originator

The portfolio's owner, usually referred to as the originator, is the seller. This portfolio is used to create asset-backed securities.

6.3.2. Special Purpose Vehicle (SPV)

The term "special purpose entity (SPE)" can also refer to a special purpose vehicle (SPV). These organizations were established to fulfill any specific business-related objectives. Typically, these SPVs are used in structured finance transactions like joint ventures, asset securitization, etc.

Different organizations, including businesses, trusts, and companies, can construct such vehicles. These organizations were established in order to organize financing. SPVs serve as the bridges between the instrument and the creator.

6.3.3. Investors

These investors may be private individuals or corporations, like mutual funds or foreign institutional investors. Assuming a position in the pool, these investors will earn interest and principal according to the parameters set forth.

6.3.4. Other Parties

Other parties are:

- **Obligor:** The originator's debtor is the obligor.
- **Servicer:** The servicer is in charge of handling all administrative tasks connected to the securitization process.
- **Trustee:** In order to safeguard the interests of numerous investors, the trustee or investor representative must behave in a guardian-like way.
- **Credit Rating Agency:** The responsibility of giving an impartial assessment of the credit risk associated with the transaction falls to the credit rating agency. Credit ratings are used to achieve this.
- **Regulators:** The regulators urge caution over a number of problems, including deal accounting approach, capital adequacy, credit quality, and liquidity.
- **Service Providers:** Credit enhancers and liquidity providers are included in the category of service providers.
- **Specialist Functionaries:** Professionals who provide specialized services, such as accountants, tax advisors, and lawyers, etc., are known as specialist functionaries.

6.4. TYPES OF SECURITIZED INSTRUMENTS

Following are the main securitized debt instruments:

- Mortgage-backed securities (MBS) which are sponsored by mortgages.

- Asset backed securities (ABS) which are sponsored by consumer debt.
- Collateralized debt obligations (CDO) which are sponsored by corporate debt including bonds.

These instruments or Types of securitized assets offer the opportunities and risks associated with their underlying assets.

6.4.1. Mortgage-Backed Securities (MBS)

Mortgage pools are used to create mortgage-backed securities (MBS). These pools are separated into a number of tranches, which are then sold. With regard to the degree of amortization, adjustable rate, payments, and other factors, the resulting security has the same rights and obligations.

Additionally, they share the same maturity date and interest rate. Mortgage payment collection is given to the originator, who subsequently transfers it to the security holders. These costs are reduced by a variety of charges and warranties (Figure 6.3).

Figure 6.3. Mortgage-backed security.

Source: Image by Public Domain Vectors.

Residential mortgages were the first type of asset to be securitized. Such mortgages continue to make up the majority of the securitization market. Residential mortgages are more suited for this type of securitization due to a number of factors, including a lower risk of value erosion through depreciation.

Following are the main characteristics of residential mortgages:

- These mortgages are medium to long-term in their duration and are more suitable for meeting the requirements of various investors.
- The receivables are uniform in nature and are therefore subject to standardized procedures because they are sponsored with their assistance.
- In the country where these mortgages were first created, the United States, the government backs such mortgages.
- These receivables are good for risk diversification since these are spread over vast geographical area.

6.4.2. Asset-Backed Securities (ABS)

The term "asset-backed securities" (ABS) refers to bonds that are constructed from various consumer debts, such as auto loans, home equity loans, and personal loans. These financial firms that provide credit for such loans treat them as assets. A corporation known as a trust, which only exists on paper, may purchase these assets after that. Such trusts only function to issue bonds with such loans serving as the security for the backing.

For instance, an auto loan could be securitized, with the loan repayments flowing to the trust and then to the investors who bought the securities backed by such loans.

6.4.3. Collateralized Debt Obligations (CDO)

Assets mostly made from non-mortgage loans are known as CDO. Debt obligation is another one of these. The terms collateralized loan obligation and collateralized bond obligation may also be used to refer to a collateralized debt obligation.

However, in certain circumstances, the security is limited to loans or bonds, as appropriate. Investors are the ones who take on the credit risk. The instruments are made available by CDO in a number of tranches, which helps to provide various levels of credit risk and maturity terms.

There are numerous types of tranches, including senior, mezzanine, and subordinate or equity. According to the degree of credit risk, such categorization is created. Senior tranches receive preference for payments in cases of default or poor performance.

Mezzanine is the following priority tier, and so forth. In general, senior, and mezzanine have ratings between A and AAA, B, and BBB. According to the grading, the underlying asset is of a certain caliber. Additionally, it displays the degree of security offered to the tranche by smaller tranches than it.

A Collateralized Debt Obligation is supported by a sponsoring company. A specific purpose vehicle for storing collateral and issuing securities, such an organization. Sponsors can include a variety of organizations, like banks or investment managers. The costs of such sponsors are subtracted from the investor payments. Additionally, these businesses keep the majority of the tranches of subordinated equity.

6.5. HOW SECURITIZATION WORKS?

In a securitization, the business holding the assets, known as the originator, compiles information on the assets it wants to remove from its related balance sheets. For example, if it were a bank, it might be doing this with a variety of mortgages and personal loans it doesn't want to service anymore. This gathered group of assets is now considered a reference portfolio.

The portfolio is subsequently sold by the creator to an issuer who will produce tradeable securities. Securities that have been created indicate a share in the portfolio's assets. For a predetermined rate of return, investors will purchase the newly minted securities.

Tranches are the several divisions that are frequently used to describe the reference portfolio, the brand-new securitized financial asset. The assets are divided into tranches based on a variety of characteristics, including the type of loans, their maturity date, their interest rates, and the amount of principle still owed.

As a result, each tranche carries different degrees of risk and offer different yields. The interest rates that less-qualified borrowers of the underlying loans pay increase in direct proportion to risk levels, and vice versa: the greater the risk, the greater the prospective rate of return.

Securitization is best shown through mortgage-backed securities (MBS). The issuer can break up the pool of mortgages after merging them into a sizable portfolio based on the individual mortgages' individual default risks. Once packaged as a certain form of bond, these smaller chunks are then sold to investors. Investors assume the role of the lender by purchasing the security. Through securitization, the initial lender or creditor can delete the related assets from its balance sheets. They can approve more loans since they have less liability on their balance sheets.

Investors profit as they earn a rate of return based on the associated principal and interest payments being made on the underlying loans and obligations by the debtors or borrowers.

6.6. BENEFITS OF SECURITIZATION

By enabling small investors to buy securities that they otherwise could not, the securitization process generates liquidity. A mortgage-backed security (MBS), for instance, allows a buyer to purchase a portion of a mortgage in exchange for regular interest and principal payments. Small investors might not have the resources to invest in a sizable pool of mortgages without the securitization of mortgages.

Many loan-based securities are backed by physical assets, unlike certain other financial instruments. If a debtor stops making loan payments on, say, his car or his house, the asset may be seized and sold to pay off individuals who have an interest in the debt.

Also, as the originator moves debt into the securitized portfolio it reduces the amount of liability held on their balance sheet. With reduced liability, they are then able to underwrite additional loans.

6.7. THE SECURITIZATION PROCESS

The procedure has two steps in its most basic form. A business with loans or other income-generating assets, known as the originator, selects the assets it wants to remove from its balance sheet and gathers them into what is known as the reference portfolio in step one.

Then it sells this pool of assets to an issuer, such as a SPV, a business normally established by a financial institution with the sole goal of acquiring the assets and realizing their off-balance-sheet treatment for tax and accounting reasons.

By issuing tradable, interest-bearing securities that are offered to capital market investors in step two, the issuer raises money for the purchase of the combined assets. A trustee account financed by the cash flows produced by the reference portfolio pays the investors at a fixed or variable rate.

In most cases, the originator services the loans in the portfolio, collects payments from the original borrowers, and passes them on—less a servicing fee—directly to the SPV or the trustee. In essence, securitization represents an alternative and diversified source of finance based on the transfer of credit risk (and possibly also interest rate and currency risk) from issuers to investors.

In a more recent improvement, the reference portfolio is broken into many slices, known as tranches, each of which has a distinct level of risk attached to it and is sold individually. Losses and investment return (principal and interest repayment) are distributed among the several tranches in accordance with their seniority.

The least risky tranche, for example, has first call on the income generated by the underlying assets, while the riskiest has last claim on that income. The conventional securitization structure assumes a three-tier security design—junior, mezzanine, and senior tranches.

With this structure, predicted portfolio losses are concentrated in the junior, or first loss position, which is typically the smallest tranche but also the one that carries the majority of the credit exposure and earns the highest return.

In senior tranches, portfolio losses are not anticipated to be significant. However, these tranches are particularly susceptible to changes in underlying asset quality because investors frequently borrow money to pay for their purchases. The troubles in the market for subprime mortgages last year were initially caused by this sensitivity.

When repayment issues surfaced in the riskiest tranches, lack of confidence spread to holders of more senior tranches—causing panic among investors and a flight into safer assets, resulting in a fire sale of securitized debt.

Mortgages and other straightforward, self-liquidating assets were the first assets for which securitization was utilized to finance. But in theory, a reference portfolio that supports securitized debt can be built out of any kind of asset with a consistent cash flow. Securities can be backed not only by mortgages but by corporate and sovereign loans, consumer credit, project finance, lease/trade receivables, and individualized lending agreements.

Although securitization transactions backed by residential or commercial mortgage loans are referred to as MBS, the generic term for such products is asset-backed securities (ABS). The same structural technique as an ABS is used in a version known as a collateralized debt obligation, which also incorporates a wider and more varied variety of assets.

6.8. THE ALLURE OF SECURITIZING

The original purpose of securitization was to help businesses and financial institutions find new sources of funding by either removing assets from their balance sheets or borrowing against them to refinance the original investment at a reasonable market rate. It reduced their borrowing costs and, in the case of banks, lowered regulatory minimum capital requirements.

For example, suppose a leasing company needed to raise cash. Under standard procedures, the company would take out a loan or sell bonds. Its ability to do so, and the cost, would depend on its overall financial health and credit rating. If it could find buyers, it could sell some of the leases directly, effectively converting a future income stream to cash.

Since there is hardly any secondary market for individual leases, this is a concern. However, by grouping those leases together, the business can raise money by offering the package to an issuer, who will then turn the group of leases into a tradable security.

Additionally, because the assets are separated from the balance sheet (and credit rating) of the originator, issuers can raise money to finance the purchase of assets at a lower cost than would be possible if they relied solely on the strength of the originator's balance sheet.

For instance, a company with an overall "B" rating with "AAA"-rated assets on its books might be able to raise funds at an "AAA" rather than "B" rating by securitizing those assets. Unlike conventional debt, securitization does not inflate a company's liabilities. Instead, it produces funds for future investment without balance sheet growth.

Securitization makes a wider variety of investable assets accessible to investors, but there are additional benefits as well. Additionally, because securitization transactions are flexible, issuers can adjust the risk-return characteristics of tranches to suit investors' risk appetites.

> For instance, beyond what may be offered by the public debt issuance by governments, pension funds and other collective investment schemes demand a wide variety of highly rated long-term fixed-income investments.

Investors can quickly and affordably alter their individual exposure to credit-sensitive assets in reaction to changes in their own risk aversion, market sentiment, and consumption choices if securitized debt is exchanged.

Sometimes the originators do not sell the securities outright to the issuer (called "true sale securitization") but instead sell only the credit risk associated with the assets without the transfer of legal title ("synthetic securitization"). Issuers can take advantage of price discrepancies between acquired assets—which are frequently illiquid—and the price investors are ready to pay for them through the use of synthetic securitization (if diversified in a greater pool of assets).

6.9. GROWTH OF SECURITIZATION

Securitization's environment has undergone a significant transformation during the past 10 years. It is no longer bound by conventional assets with predetermined conditions, such mortgages, bank loans, or consumer loans (called self-liquidating assets).

Improved modeling and risk quantification as well as greater data availability have encouraged issuers to consider a wider variety of asset types, including home equity loans, lease receivables, and small business loans, to name a few.

Even though the majority of issuance is concentrated in mature markets, securitization has seen significant growth in emerging markets, where large, well-regarded corporate entities and banks have used it to convert future cash flow from hard-currency export receivables or remittances into current cash.

Securitized products are going to get easier in the future. Issuers will soon be confronted with regulatory reforms that will demand greater capital charges and more thorough valuation after recording little capital reserves on highly rated securitized debt for years.

It might also be necessary for issuers to maintain interest in the performance of all senior tranches of securitized assets, not only the junior tranche, to revive securitization operations and regain investor confidence.

6.10. ADVANTAGES OF SECURITIZATION

The main benefits of the process of debt securitization are discussed in subsections.

6.10.1. Benefits to Issuers/Originator

Since it offers a practical and economical source of capital, securitization benefits the issuer. It assists in turning capital-intensive assets into capital-efficient ones. Fees and levies are also used to create additional money.

- **Diversification and Reduction in Cost of Funding:** The originators' revenue streams can be diversified with the aid of securitization. It aids in lowering funding costs as well. For instance, the cost of issuing corporate bonds is higher than the cost of raising money through securitization.
- **Management of Regulatory Capital:** The management of risk-based capital requirements can also be accomplished through asset securitization. This idea is well-liked in developed markets like those in the US and Europe. The usage of securitization as a management tool is anticipated to advance along with the rising deregulation.
- **Generation of Servicing Fee Income:** With asset securitization, the issuer can utilize capital-intensive assets to their fullest potential. It helps to increase different fees like the origination fee and the service cost without changing the capital base of the company in a proportional way. Usually, this is accomplished by securitizing the debt and selling it after. But the company itself keeps the servicing portion.
- To provide general services, the servicing charge is used. Additionally, it is utilized to transfer funds to the issue's servicer, who serves as the payment agent for the issue's securitized assets. Due to their existing infrastructure, financial institutions may benefit from securitization in these circumstances.
- **Management of Interest Rate Volatility:** Securitization aids businesses in controlling interest rate volatility. A financial institution's finances may be severely impacted by a negative change in interest rates.

  In such circumstances, the institutions may securitize the more erratic assets, while the company may choose to hold onto the other assets for the purpose of enhancing its asset and liability position. Thus, in such cases, the financial institutions act both as an issuer as well as an investor.

6.10.2. Benefits to Investors

Securitization helps in turning fixed assets into liquid sources of funds. It helps in reducing credit risk as:

- These are backed by a vast collection of loans.

- It leads to credit enhancement, which is a financial tool for reducing the credit risk.
- It helps the investors in diversifying their investment avenues.
- It also helps in reducing costs of inter-mediation and thus improves the returns.

6.10.3. Benefits to Borrowers

Due to the fact that either a financial or non-financial company can securitize the loans it has generated, the issuer benefits from increased liquidity when selling such securitized assets. His need for capital is met in part by this. It aids in closing the interest gap as well. Spread arising from Treasury bonds and leading rates as securities. In the market for mortgages, this is common.

The auto loan market is now seeing the trend as well. As the market improves, more originators might turn to securitization, which would result in a decrease in the market's interest spreads. Such business dealings have a positive impact on profits and can expand to other markets.

6.11. WHAT ROLE DID SECURITIZATION PLAY IN THE GLOBAL FINANCIAL CRISIS (GFC)?

Securitization, specifically the packaging of mortgage debt into bond-like financial instruments, was a key driver of the 2007–2008 global financial crisis (GFC). When the U.S. real estate bubble burst, securitization encouraged excessive risk-taking that led to the collapse of numerous significant Wall Street and international financial institutions. Packaging of assets into a financial product is known as securitization.

The securitization of mortgage debt, particularly subprime mortgages, in MBS and CDO, was a major cause of both the U.S. real estate bubble in the early and mid-2000s and the financial havoc that resulted from the popping of that bubble.

Banks and other lenders who provided borrowers with mortgages then sold those mortgages to larger banks for repackaging into MBS and CDOs.

6.11.1. Mortgage Securitization and Risk

As time went on, the lenders who issued the loans were no longer at danger if the homeowner failed because they had transferred the loans to major banks for securitization. As a result, lending criteria drastically decreased.

This meant that a lot of unqualified or underqualified borrowers, sometimes known as subprime borrowers, were able to obtain dangerous loans.

Subprime mortgages eventually contributed to the MBS and CDOs' attractiveness to large investors since they produced better returns because of the higher interest rates subprime borrowers were required to pay. The assets continually got excellent ratings from credit rating agencies, and at the same time it was thought that bundling would lower investors' risk.

So, the assets were used as leverage to control many trillions of dollars—many times the face value of the underlying assets.

This situation was highly profitable to everyone as the real estate market boomed, with buyers aggressively bidding up the prices of available houses. Places such as California, Florida, Arizona, and Las Vegas saw astronomical home-price increases as more and more easy money flooded in the market.

Subprime borrowers initially had two options when they fell behind on their payments: they could restructure their mortgages using a greater property valuation, or they could sell their homes for a quick profit. If prices were increasing, the level of risk in the system was unimportant.

By 2005, subprime mortgages represented a third of the total mortgage market, up from 10% only two years earlier. After the economy started to sputter and housing prices started to fall, things started to shift. Mortgage delinquencies increased and adjustable-rate mortgages (ARMs) already had started to reset at higher rates.

By March 2007, the value of subprime mortgages had reached around $1.3 trillion. A little more than a year later, in July 2008, more than a fifth of subprime mortgages were delinquent, and 29% of ARMs were seriously delinquent.

The mortgage-backed assets held by banks were in serious difficulties and desperately trying to be sold as the value of their securities plunged as a result of the collapse of the housing market. The global economic downturn was in full force.

6.12. APPLICATION OF DEBT SECURITIZATION

- **Creation of Marketable Securities:** Making marketable securities out of non-tradable items is possible with the help of the securitization process. In order to provide liquidity and transferability, this transformation is primarily being undertaken.

For businesses with sizable quantities of receivables shown as assets on their balance sheets, this is particularly crucial.

The main characteristic for an instrument to be suitable for securitization is that it should be repayable over a defined period of time. Such payments should also be certain House mortgages and car leases fulfill these criterions. In present day, utility companies, insurance companies, aviation sector, etc., is also moving towards securitization.

- **Identification of Cash Flows:** The process of securitization aids in the conversion of financial claims into tradeable securities. Potential cash flows and claims against third parties are transformed into tradeable securities as part of the process. These claims are located, gathered, and then divided into tranches that are sold to investors.
- **Securitization of Receivables:** The concept of securitization is used in this situation as a prime illustration. Typically, the securitization of a claim against an issuer occurs. A claim against the issuing corporation arises, for instance, when a debenture is issued. The claim against the third party, however, is what is being securitized in the instance of securitizing receivables. Thus, the investor gets the recourse to the debtor of the originator.
- **Funding Alternatives:** The process of securitization also involves debtors. This fact adds unique dimension to the process.
- According to the law, it is possible for a claim against a third party to become a tradeable instrument. It is a truth that an entity has the ability to produce a marketable instrument for a claim on itself. The situation is different, though, when the claims against third parties are transformed into tradable securities.

  The procedure gives the issuers the opportunity to create a product that closely resembles the supporting asset, which gives them a distinct advantage. The securities are unrelated to the issuer's commitment. Consequently, the issuer's credit rating is not very significant for these instruments.
- **Re-Allocation of Risks:** Credit risk can be transferred to investors by securitization, which is beneficial. By allowing the originator to take on greater risk through greater exposure, it further helps the process. In order to move market risk, securitization is also helpful. These dangers include those associated with interest

rates, liquidity, or prepayment. It also reduces the requirement for risk capital, which further helps in better pricing of the backing assets.

- **Balance Sheet Management:** Securitization assists in releasing the originator's capital. Due to the addition of a new asset class to the balance sheet, it also aids in lowering debt after a securitized sale. Securitization could produce matching money for the assets on the balance sheet. Additionally, it aids in the sale of non-core assets through proper structuring.

6.13. THE GLOBAL FINANCIAL CRISIS (GFC) 2008

6.13.1. Financial Crimes

The Federal Bureau of Investigation (FBI) investigates matters relating to fraud, theft, or embezzlement occurring within or against the national and international financial community. These offenses are defined by dishonesty, concealment, or breach of trust and do not require the use or threat of physical force or violence.

Such acts are committed by individuals and organizations to obtain personal or business advantage. The FBI focuses its financial crimes investigations on such criminal activities as corporate fraud, securities, and commodities fraud, health care fraud, financial institution fraud, mortgage fraud, insurance fraud, mass marketing fraud, and money laundering. These are the identified priority crime problem areas of the financial crimes section (FCS) of the FBI.

The FCS's mandate is to supervise financial fraud investigations and to make it easier to seize assets from people who commit federal offenses. In fiscal year (FY) 2009, the FCS is comprised of the Asset Forfeiture (AF)/ money laundering unit (MLU), the Economic Crimes Unit, the Health Care Fraud Unit, and the National Mortgage Fraud Team.

The Economic Crimes Unit is responsible for significant frauds targeted against individuals, businesses, and industries to include corporate fraud, insurance fraud (non-health care related), securities, and commodities fraud, mass marketing fraud, telemarketing fraud, high yield investment schemes, Ponzi schemes, advance fees schemes, and pyramid schemes.

Investigations directed at people or organizations that are abusing the public and private health care systems are supervised by the Health Care

Fraud Unit. Areas investigated under health care fraud include billing for services not rendered, billing for a higher reimbursable service than performed (upcoding), performing unnecessary services, kickbacks, unbundling of tests and services to generate higher fees, durable medical equipment fraud, pharmaceutical drug diversion, outpatient surgery fraud, and Internet pharmacy sales.

The National Mortgage Fraud Team's goal is to track down and destroy criminal groups and individuals who perpetrate fraud schemes against financial institutions, notably in the fields of mortgage fraud and bank failures.

Regarding financial institution fraud, the mission of the AF/MLU is to identify, target, disrupt, and dismantle criminal organizations and individuals through the strategic use of AF. It also involves making sure that field offices use the money laundering violation in all investigations, as necessary, to help disrupt and/or dismantle criminal enterprises.

The AF/MLU also has responsibilities for the management of the forfeiture support project (FSP) in Calverton, Maryland. Although the FSP's mission is closely tied to that of AF/MLU, it does have a separate mission statement which is documented as follows. With the help of data entry, financial document analysis, forensic accounting, and asset tracking, the FSP supports the forfeiture component of all significant FBI investigations.

Based upon field office crime surveys, current trends in the white collar crime arena, and directives established by the president, the attorney general, the Director, and the Criminal Investigative Division, the following national priorities for the white collar crime program (WCCP) have been established: public corruption, corporate fraud/securities fraud, health care fraud, financial institution fraud (to include bank failures and mortgage fraud), money laundering, insurance fraud and mass marketing fraud.

Although it is a top concern for the WCCP on a national level, public corruption will not be included in this report. This report's sections give an overview, statistical highlights, and real-world examples of the top criminal issues that the FCS is focusing on in each section. To prevent the public from becoming a victim of fraud, recommendations are provided when necessary.

6.13.2. Corporate Fraud

The FBI has concentrated its efforts on instances involving accounting fraud, corporate officer self-dealing, and obstruction of justice as the leading agency looking into corporate fraud. Most incidents of corporate fraud that the FBI investigates include accounting fraud, which is the practice of misleading investors, auditors, and analysts about a company's genuine financial situation.

A corporation's share price can be fraudulently boosted by manipulating financial data based on false performance metrics that are disclosed to the investing public. Corporate fraud can harm the American economy and investor trust in addition to causing investors to suffer huge financial losses.

The FBI has recently noticed a rise in the number of corporate fraud cases involving subprime lending institutions, brokerage houses, home building companies, hedge funds, and financial institutions because of the financial crisis, which was partly brought on by the collapse of the subprime market in the fall of 2007.

As a result of the current financial crisis, trillions of dollars in shareholder value have been lost; several prominent companies, i.e., Lehman Brothers, have gone out of business; several prominent banks, i.e., IndyMac Bank and Washington Mutual, have failed; and the federal government has provided over a trillion dollars in relief to keep other companies from failing, i.e., American Insurance Group, General Motors, and Citi Group (Figure 6.4).

Figure 6.4. Washington mutual office.

Source: Image by Wikimedia Commons.

A company that provides credit to borrowers who are not eligible for loans from traditional lenders is known as a sub-prime lender. Following their issuance, subprime loans are packaged and marketed as securities, a process known as securitization. The loan procedure has been plagued by fraud, which starts when the borrower gives the mortgage broker and/or lender fraudulent information.

The next layer of potential fraud – corporate fraud – occurs with the banks, brokerage houses, and other financial institutions that package loans through the securitization process. As the housing market declined, sub-prime lenders have been forced to buy back a number of non-performing loans.

To enable the borrowers to refinance or sell their houses before entering default, many of these sub-prime lenders have relied on an ongoing rise in real estate values. Loan defaults grew, the secondary market for subprime loans securities shrank, and the securities lost value as a result of the slowdown in home sales.

As a result, publicly traded stocks dramatically decreased in value as financial institutions realized large losses due to the sub-prime securities they held or insured, resulting in financial difficulties and bankruptcies.

Figure 6.5. U.S. Department of Justice.

Source: Image by Wikimedia Commons.

Financial analyzes of publicly traded corporations have found instances of erroneous accounting entries and fraudulently inflated assets and revenues as they experienced financial difficulties as a result of the sub-prime market. Investigations have revealed that several of these businesses inflated their financial reports by manipulating the risks associated with their claimed loan portfolios.

Additionally, executives with insider knowledge sold their ownership interests and made unlawful profits before the value of the stocks of these companies fell sharply. The FBI is working with the U.S. Department of Justice (DOJ), the U.S. Securities and Exchange Commission (SEC) and other U.S. regulatory agencies to identify possible corporate fraud centered on violations of insider trading, securities fraud, and accounting fraud (Figure 6.5).

Along with the sub-prime market problem, corporate fraud cases involving executive seal-dealing, especially when corporations are used to conduct significant Ponzi fraud schemes, continue to be a source of worry. In the past, Ponzi schemes were mostly conducted by lone individuals or small groups in a communal setting.

However, the current financial crisis has revealed a number of sizable Ponzi schemes that were carried out not on a local level by individuals, but rather on a corporate level at the federal level by executives of what were once thought to be reliable investment brokerages, such as Bernard L. Madoff Investment Services LLC.

Corporate fraud remains the highest priority of the FCS and the FBI is committed to dealing with this significant crime problem. As of the end of FY 2008, 545 corporate fraud cases are being pursued by FBI field offices throughout the U.S., several of which involve losses to public investors that individually exceed $1 billion.

6.13.3. Securities and Commodities Fraud

It is now easier than ever for investors to diversify their portfolios and for U.S. firms to access finance thanks to the ongoing integration of the world's capital markets. More Americans are choosing to invest in the securities and commodities markets, whether through retirement accounts or college savings plans.

In fact, the SEC suggests that the number of people investing in securities and commodities has increased 600% since 1980. However, this rapid expansion of large-scale investments has also been accompanied by a sharp rise in the incidence of fraud and other unethical behavior in these markets. In addition, the present financial crisis has made widespread fraud schemes that have been flourishing in the global banking system more obvious. Ponzi schemes and investment frauds are not new in the current climate, but they are becoming more visible due to market decline and the instability of the American economy. In response to government initiatives intended to promote the financial markets, additional avenues for fraud have also emerged.

The FBI anticipates new iterations of traditional fraud schemes to develop as a result of the government spending programs such as the troubled asset relief program (TARP) and the termed asset-backed securities loan facility (TALF). As such, the combating of securities and commodities frauds remains a priority for the FBI's WCCP.

The losses are related to the declining market value of firms, the diminished or non-existent return on investments, and the costs of litigation and investigations. Financial institutions, public, and private businesses, governmental organizations, and retirement funds are among the victims of securities and commodities frauds.

The rigorous execution of laws and regulations intended to guarantee the fair and orderly operation of the capital markets is more important than ever for the health of the global economy. The FBI is not only aware of this crucial demand, but it is also in a unique position to support the American government's criminal investigation obligations in this field.

To look into and stop fraudulent activities in the securities markets, the FBI closely collaborates with numerous public and private organizations. Many FBI field offices run task forces and working groups with other law enforcement and regulatory agencies in an effort to strengthen these connections and meet workforce requirements.

These agencies include the SEC, U.S. Attorneys' Offices (USAO), Commodities Futures Trading Commission (CFTC), National Association of Securities Dealers (NASD), U.S. Postal Inspection Service (USPIS), and the Internal Revenue Service (IRS). Cooperation among agencies helps the FBI address the problem of securities and commodities fraud more effectively and allows the FBI to more efficiently allocate its resources.

As of the end of FY 2008, the FBI was investigating 1,210 cases of securities and commodities fraud and had as many as 150 special agents assigned to addressing this crime problem. Following are brief descriptions of some of the most prevalent types of fraud being encountered today:

- **Market Manipulation:** These popularly known "pump and dump" scams work by inducing artificial buying demand for a particular security, typically a low trading volume issuer in the over the counter (OTC) securities market that is mostly governed by the fraudsters.

This artificially increased trading volume has the effect of artificially increasing the price of the targeted security (i.e., the "pump"), which is rapidly sold off into the inflated market for the security by the fraud perpetrators (i.e., the "dump"); resulting in illicit gains to the perpetrators and losses to innocent third-party investors.

The higher trading volume is typically produced by persuading unaware investors to buy shares of the targeted securities through dishonest or fraudulent sales tactics and/or public information releases.

In a more recent iteration of these scams, foreign-based computer thieves acquire unauthorized access to and break into the online brokerage accounts of unwary victims in the United States.

The pump element of the manipulation is then carried out via these hacked victim accounts, while the dump portion is carried out by the fraudsters selling their current holdings in the targeted asset into the inflated market.

- **High Yield Investment Fraud:** High yield investment fraud schemes come in a variety of shapes and sizes, but they are all distinguished by promises of low- or no-risk investments with outlandishly high rates of return. The following schemes are the most typical among this sort of fraud:
- **The Ponzi Scheme:** Named after its early 20th-century creator, Charles Ponzi, these schemes use money collected from new 'investors' (i.e., victims), rather than profits from the purported underlying business venture, to pay the high rates of return promised to earlier victims.

  This structure gives victims the idea that the offender is running a genuine business while in reality, victim money is the only source of income.
- **The Pyramid Scheme:** Like Ponzi schemes, the money obtained from the fraud's later victims is distributed to the earlier ones to give the scheme a false air of legality. However, in pyramid schemes, victims are paid recruitment commissions in order to convince them to find other victims.
- **Prime Bank Scheme:** Victims are persuaded to invest in financial instruments issued by reputable institutions that offer risk-free opportunities for high rates of return; these benefits are

purportedly attained because the perpetrator has access to a secret global exchange that is typically only accessible to the largest financial institutions in the world.

- **Advance Fee Fraud:** This category of fraud encompasses a broad variety of schemes which are designed to induce their victims into remitting up-front payments in exchange for the promise of goods, services, and/or prizes.

  Victims of commodities and securities fraud are frequently told that they must first pay a number of taxes and/or fees in order to take part in an attractive investment opportunity. The report's section on mass marketing fraud includes more information on advance fee scam schemes.

- **Hedge Fund Fraud:** Private investment partnerships known as hedge funds have historically exclusively taken on high-net-worth clients willing to make sizable minimum initial commitments. The business as a whole has mainly remained unregulated, but middle-class investors have become more interested in it as a result of their exposure to hedge fund activities through ancillary investments (e.g., pension funds).

  The relative lack of regulatory scrutiny has made the industry vulnerable to fraud by fund managers, to include overstatement/misappropriation of fund assets; overcharging for fund management fees; insider trading; market timing; and late trading.

- **Commodities Fraud:** The sale of commodities investments by fraud or deception is a common component of these schemes. In these situations, the employment of fraudulent or deceptive sales tactics is done to obtain money from the victims for the purchase of commodities that either never happen or don't match the initial sales pitches.

  Alternately, participants in the commodities market may try to illegally manipulate the market for a commodity by taking measures like cornering the market or publishing pricing information that isn't accurate in order to artificially raise the price of the targeted commodity.

- **Foreign Exchange (FX) Fraud:** These schemes are characterized by the use of false or deceptive sales practices, alleging high rates of return for minimal risk, to induce victims to invest in the foreign currency exchange market.

In these situations, the promoted transactions either never happen, don't match the initial sales pitches, or are carried out just to earn exorbitant trading commissions in violation of fiduciary duties to the hapless client.

As an alternative, dishonest currency traders working for major financial organizations may try to manipulate FX rates in order to make unreported trading profits for their personal benefit.

- **Broker Embezzlement:** In these schemes, brokers steal directly from their clients through illegal and unauthorized operations. Forgery of client documents, falsifying account statements, unlawful trading, or fund transfers, as well as other actions that violate the broker's fiduciary duties to the hapless client, may all be used to support such schemes.
- **Late-Day Trading:** In these scams, stocks are illegally bought and sold outside of regular market hours. To prevent people from making money off of market-moving information disclosed after regular trading has ended, such trading is forbidden.

  Unscrupulous traders try to take advantage of these chances unlawfully by purchasing or selling shares at the market close price, confident that the market-moving information will result in illegal profits when trading resumes the following day.

6.13.4. Mortgage Fraud

The earliest indications of a nationwide mortgage crisis were visible as early as December 2006, when there was a noticeable increase in mortgage loan payment defaults. It was evident that the mortgage crisis had started and would worsen as the real estate market started to fall and delinquencies and foreclosure rates kept rising, especially among sub-quality borrowers.

As a result, a number of prestigious and historic financial institutions throughout the world either collapsed or needed substantial government financial assistance during 2008.

It became clear that hazardous mortgage lending practices and subprime loans made in the United States contributed negatively to the financial crisis and general economic collapse. The current financial crisis has made widespread fraud schemes, which have been flourishing in the global banking system, more obvious. Mortgage fraud schemes employ some type of "material misstatement, misrepresentation, or omission relating to the property or potential mortgage relied on by an underwriter or lender to fund, purchase, or insure a loan." The FBI compiles data on mortgage fraud through suspicious activity reports (SARs) filed by federally insured financial institutions, reports received from the Department of Housing and Urban Development-Office of the Inspector General (HUD-OIG), and complaints received from the public and mortgage industry at large.

While a major sector of the mortgage business is devoid of any mandated fraud reporting requirements and there is currently no single location where all complaints of mortgage fraud can be gathered, SARs from financial institutions have shown a marked increase in mortgage fraud reporting.

For example, during FY 2008, mortgage fraud SARs increased more than 36% to 63,173. The total dollar loss attributed to mortgage fraud is unknown since only 7% of SARs filed during FY 2008 indicated a specific dollar loss, which totaled more than $1.5 billion.

The time wait between finding a problematic loan, selling the property through foreclosure, and then figuring out the loss amount is the reason that only 7% of SARs reported a financial loss.

The review of SARs helps the FBI launch a lot of its investigations into mortgage fraud. In reality, the FBI has created a variety of new analysis techniques to further utilize the enormous volumes of intelligence included in SARs.

All other FBI investigative and intelligence programs have been improved as a result of the benefits, in addition to the Mortgage Fraud Program specifically. When it comes to exchanging analytic techniques and trend information derived from SARs, the FBI, and financial crimes enforcement network (FinCEN) collaborate closely.

From March 1, 2008, to June 18, 2008, the FBI and DOJ orchestrated a national mortgage fraud takedown named operation malicious mortgage (OMM) that was announced on June 19, 2008. OMM primarily addressed three types of mortgage fraud schemes: lending fraud, foreclosure rescue scams, and mortgage-related bankruptcy schemes.

OMM resulted in 144 mortgage fraud cases in which 406 defendants were charged for their involvement in mortgage fraud schemes that resulted in an estimated $1.07 billion in losses. Charges were brought in every region of the U.S. and in more than 50 judicial districts by USAO based upon the law enforcement and investigative efforts of participating law enforcement agencies. In addition to the FBI, these agencies included IRS-CI, USPIS, U.S. Secret Service, U.S. Immigration and Customs Enforcement, HUD-

OIG, Federal Deposit Insurance Corporation-Office of the Inspector General (FDIC-OIG), and the Department of Veterans Affairs-Office of the Inspector General.

Operation Continued Action (COM) in 2004 and operation quick flip (QF) in 2005 were two previous coordinated sweeps in an ongoing law enforcement operation to address mortgage fraud.

Mortgage fraud is a subject of two separate FBI investigations: fraud for profit and fraud for housing. The goal of profit-driven fraud, often known as "industry insider fraud," is to move equity, artificially inflate the value of the property, or offer loans based on phony properties.

A significant portion of all documented fraud losses involve collaboration or participation by industry insiders, according to ongoing investigations and mortgage fraud reporting. Fraud for housing refers to wrongdoings that the borrower alone committed.

The primary goal of this fraud is to obtain and retain ownership of a home through deception. When a borrower lies about his income or employment history in order to get approved for a loan, it is considered this sort of fraud.

Despite the substantial number of mortgage fraud schemes, the FBI is concentrating its efforts on those that are carried out by industry insiders. The FBI's involvement in the mortgage sector focuses mostly on public awareness campaigns and the identification of fraud patterns. Equity theft, real estate flipping, and mortgage-related identity theft are a few of the recent mortgage fraud schemes that law enforcement has come across.

Utilizing corporate shell firms, stealing corporate identities, and using bankruptcy or the fear of foreclosure to deceive homeowners and investors are all common equity skimming techniques. An educated criminal element is posing a challenge to law enforcement, using identity theft, straw borrowers, shell businesses, and business insiders to hide their techniques and circumvent lender regulations.

Property flipping is best described as purchasing properties and artificially inflating their value through false appraisals. The artificially valued properties are then repurchased several times for a higher price by associates of the "flipper." After several sham sales, the properties are foreclosed on by victim lenders.

Mortgage fraud should not be contrasted with predatory lending practices, which mostly harm borrowers. Typically, aged citizens, people with low incomes, and people with bad credit are the victims of predatory lending.

Predatory lending pushes borrowers to pay exorbitant loan origination/settlement fees, subprime or higher interest rates, and occasionally unfair service fees. When this occurs, the borrower frequently misses payments on their mortgage, which may lead to foreclosure or forced refinancing.

The FBI has also seen the following emerging schemes associated with the downturn of the financial markets during 2008: builder-bailout, short-sale, and foreclosure rescue scams.

A builder-bailout scheme can occur when a builder or developer experiences difficulty selling their inventory and resorts to using fraudulent means to unload them, such as excessive incentives to buyers that are not disclosed on the mortgage loan documents.

In a real estate short sale, the lender consents to sell the property for less than the mortgage balance owing. Short sales are becoming more and more common in the currently fast decreasing U.S. housing market as banks are forced to take on an increasing number of properties through the formal foreclosure procedure.

In a short sale fraud scheme, the perpetrator buys a house using a fictitious buyer who then defaults on the loan, resulting in a short sale that the perpetrator may then take advantage of and buy at a deep discount.

Criminals that prey on honest homeowners in desperate financial situations and defraud them of payments for foreclosure protection services or ownership stakes in residential properties are known as "foreclosure rescue scammers."

The number of foreclosure rescue scams that prey on unwary victims has increased as foreclosures across the nation continue to grow. These criminals will claim to help struggling homes, but they frequently exacerbate the situation by taking no action at all.

For instance, the homeowner might be giving the offender rent while the offender makes up stories about paying the mortgage or negotiating with the lender. Other times, the offender will conceal their actions by using counterfeit and altered deeds to either sell the house or obtain a second loan on it.

The FBI is working with other law enforcement and regulatory partners, as well as industry liaisons to target, disrupt, and dismantle the criminal organizations and/or individuals engaging in these fraud schemes.

In FY 2008, there are 16 mortgage fraud task forces and 38 working groups in the country. With representatives of federal, state, and local law enforcement, these task forces are strategically placed in areas identified as high threat areas for mortgage fraud. Partners are varied, but typically include representatives of the IRS-CID, USPIS, HUD-OIG, FDIC-OIG, as well as state and local law enforcement officers across the country.

Although the FBI has increased the number of agents investigating mortgage fraud cases across the nation, this multi-agency model acts as a force multiplier by offering a variety of resources to adequately identify the source of the fraud and find the best way to prosecute each case, especially in active markets where fraud is common.

The FBI also collaborates closely with individual lenders and national organizations including the Mortgage Bankers Association, the National Association of Mortgage Brokers, the Appraisal Institute, and the National Notary Association to define and address the mortgage fraud issue.

Regional analysis of SARs indicating mortgage fraud violations shows that the western region of the U.S. led the nation with 38% of mortgage fraud-related SARs filed during FY 2008. South-eastern, north central, north-eastern, and south-central regions had 25%, 19%, 12%, and 6%, respectively of mortgage fraud-related SAR filings.

However, FBI pending cases indicated the north central region had the majority of mortgage fraud cases with 27%, during 2008. The western, north-eastern, south-eastern, and south-central regions had 24%, 19%, 16%, and 14%, respectively.

6.14. CONCLUSION

The GFC is discussed in this chapter's summary of securitization and financial crime. Securitization, its background, and the parties involved in securitization have been covered at length in the introduction to this chapter. The types of securitized instruments and the mechanism of securitization are also explained in this chapter.

This chapter also discusses the advantages of securitization, the securitization process, the rise of securitization, and the benefits of securitization towards the middle of the chapter. This chapter also aids in understanding how securitization contributed to the world financial crisis. Towards the end of this chapter, applications of debt securitization and the GFC of 2008 have been discussed.

REFERENCES

1. Chen, J., (2022). *Securitization: Definition, Pros & Cons, Examples*. Investopedia. Available at: https://www.investopedia.com/terms/s/securitization.asp (accessed on 15 June 2023).
2. *Financial Crimes 2008,* (2010). FBI. Available at: https://www.fbi.gov/stats-services/publications/fcs_report2008 (accessed on 15 June 2023).
3. Senarath, S. L., (2019). *Securitization in Light of the Global Financial Crisis: Towards an Optimal Regulatory Framework with Special, Home*. Griffith University. Available at: https://research-repository.griffith.edu.au/handle/10072/367515 (accessed on 15 June 2023).
4. Solanki, K., (2022). *Securitization: Definition, Types, Benefits, Instruments, Application & Mechanism of Debt Securitization*. Top4u. Blogger. Available at: https://www.toppers4u.com/2022/03/securitization-definition-types.html (accessed on 15 June 2023).
5. Team, T. I., (2021). *What Role Did Securitization Play in the Global Financial Crisis?* Investopedia. Available at: https://www.investopedia.com/ask/answers/041515/what-role-did-securitization-play-us-subprime-mortgage-crisis.asp (accessed on 15 June 2023).
6. *What is Securitization?* – International Monetary Fund, (n.d.). Available at: https://www.imf.org/external/pubs/ft/fandd/2008/09/pdf/basics.pdf (accessed on 15 June 2023).

CHAPTER 7

Virtual Currency in a Virtual World

Contents

This chapter talks about Virtual Currency in a virtual world. At the beginning of the chapter, this chapter explains about the introduction and types of virtual currencies. The chapter also addresses the Advantages of virtual currencies, the Disadvantages of virtual currencies, Differences between digital currencies, Virtual currencies, and Cryptocurrencies. The chapter provides highlights on the Bitcoin and store of value money function, Virtual currency concerns, and Regulatory implications.

7.1. INTRODUCTION

A digital value representation known as a virtual currency is one that is exclusively accessible digitally. Application-specific software, mobile, or computer programs are used to store and trade with it. Virtual currency transactions happen through the Internet or on secure, dedicated networks. They are unregulated and issued by individual parties or groups of developers.

Digital currencies of various kinds, like cryptocurrencies and tokens issued by private companies, are grouped together as virtual currencies, which are a subset of all digital currencies. Faster transaction times and simplicity of usage are two advantages of virtual currency. Virtual currencies' drawbacks include their vulnerability to hacking and the fact that, because they are unregulated, they do not offer investors many legal protections.

Virtual currencies are a form of digital currency. They do not have a physical manifestation like paper money; instead, they are issued by private parties, such as a group of developers or organizations, and are only meant for use online. Thus, they are different from digital representations of central bank-issued currency, also known as central bank digital currency (CBDC).

The term virtual currency came into existence in 2012, when the European Central Bank (ECB) defined it to classify types of "digital money in an unregulated environment, issued, and controlled by its developers and used as a payment method among members of a specific virtual community."

The Internal Revenue Service (IRS) in the United States describes virtual currencies as "digital representations of value that function as a unit of account, a store of value, and a medium of exchange."

Although these definitions are sufficiently broad to cover a variety of characteristics of virtual currencies, they might not be totally accurate at this time.

Since 2012, a wide range of currencies that do not fit the ECB's definition of the term have been added to the list of possible virtual currencies. For example, certain cryptocurrencies, which are considered a form of virtual currency, like Ripple's XRP, are not strictly controlled or used by a virtual community.

Virtual currencies have also been unsuccessful in being widely accepted as a form of payment or a means of exchange. They occasionally used, sometimes as a speculative financial asset and other times in gaming groups. It is also uncertain whether they have become a store of value comparable to gold.

Additionally, there is the issue of regulation. Although virtual currencies are still not regulated in the vast majority of financial jurisdictions, this is slowly starting to change. Bitcoin, the cryptocurrency with the biggest market capitalization, is legal tender in El Salvador.

Virtual currencies are unregulated in the United States, which has the most sophisticated financial markets in the world. However, authorities are seriously considering regulation. The Securities Regulator and Exchange Commission (SEC) intends to regulate cryptocurrency exchanges.

Another type of virtual currency that is slated for regulation is stable coins. The IRS levies taxes on transactions involving specific virtual currencies, including cryptocurrency.

7.2. TYPES OF VIRTUAL CURRENCIES

Depending on their operating network, virtual currencies are classified as subsections (Figure 7.1).

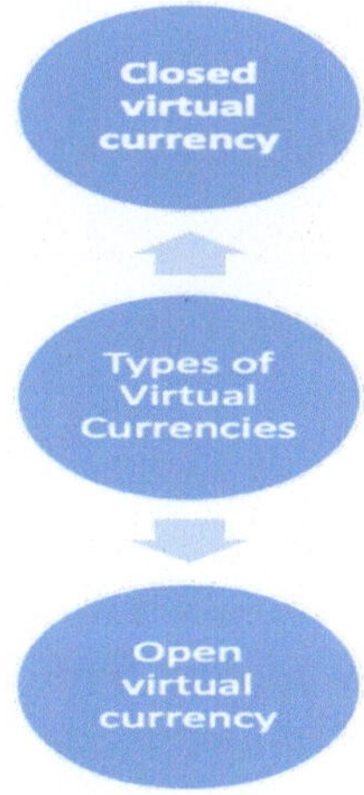

Figure 7.1. *Types of virtual currencies.*

7.2.1. Closed Virtual Currency

As the name implies, a closed virtual currency functions in a regulated and private ecosystem. It cannot be changed into a fiat currency from the real world or into another virtual currency. For instance, virtual money used in gaming systems is closed.

Despite being usable in their particular contexts (in this case, video games), such currencies cannot be exchanged for actual money. Another example of closed virtual currencies is airline miles. Private parties issue them, can only purchase additional miles, and cannot be converted into their associated monetary value.

7.2.2. Open Virtual Currency

The fact that open virtual currencies can be exchanged for other types of money gives them the name convertible virtual currencies. They function in open ecosystems and are convertible into other currencies both inside and outside of the platform. Examples of open virtual currencies are stable coins and cryptocurrencies.

The two most valuable cryptocurrencies, Bitcoin, and Ethereum, can be changed into other cryptocurrencies or specific fiat currencies. The IRS classifies this conversion process as a commerce transaction and levies tax on it.

Although most open virtual currencies are decentralized, some, like Ripple's XRP, are designed to be centralized, which means a central organization is in charge of their production and distribution.

7.3. ADVANTAGES OF VIRTUAL CURRENCIES

The advantages of virtual currencies are as follows:

- Virtual currencies do not have expensive manufacturing and physical storage costs.
- The technology rails of virtual currencies increase transaction speeds and eliminate geographical boundaries.
- When used in financial transactions, decentralized virtual currencies can do away with middlemen and create a direct link between the two parties involved.
- It is possible to program virtual currencies to conduct automatic transactions. For instance, without requiring human interaction,

smart contracts on Ethereum's block chain can retain and distribute funds from escrow accounts.

- In the digital world, virtual currencies serve as value repositories and can be used to value a variety of items, including artwork and game tokens.

7.4. DISADVANTAGES OF VIRTUAL CURRENCIES

The disadvantages of virtual currencies are as follows:

- Hackers are drawn to virtual currencies as lucrative targets. Numerous instances of block chain networks, a type of virtual currency, being hacked have occurred.
- Though they do not have manufacturing or physical storage costs, virtual currencies have other associated expenses. For example, cryptocurrency users are required to store them in digital wallets. At trading exchanges, cryptocurrencies also have custody costs.
- Scams can occur using virtual money. Several initial coin offers (ICOs), which gained popularity after a spike in cryptocurrency prices, were essentially frauds where private developers sold worthless tokens for fictitious networks. A currency exchange was not possible with the tokens.
- Due to the fact that unregulated virtual currencies are issued by private organizations and, for the most part, are not governed by financial authorities, investors do not have legal recourse.

  Virtual currencies traded on exchanges, such as cryptocurrencies, can be subject to highly volatile price swings.

7.5. DIFFERENCES BETWEEN DIGITAL CURRENCIES, VIRTUAL CURRENCIES, AND CRYPTOCURRENCIES

Even though they sound alike and function in a similar manner, digital, virtual, and cryptocurrencies are in fact different. Listed below are the main points of difference between the three types of currencies (Figure 7.2):

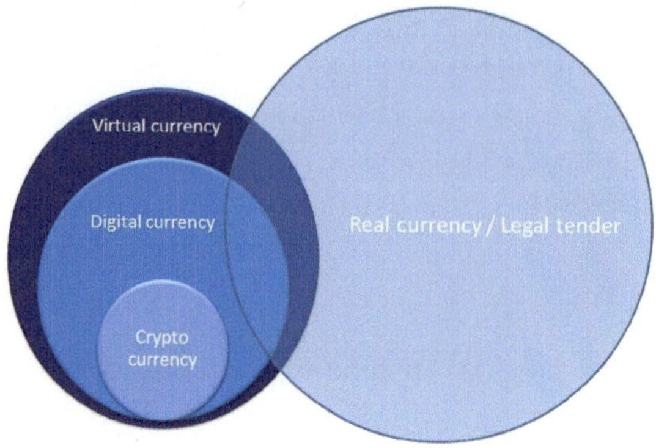

Figure 7.2. Virtual currency relationship.

Source: Image by Wikimedia Commons.

- Digital currencies include all types of virtual money including cryptocurrency. But not all digital currencies fall within those two headings. For example, CBDCs are not virtual currencies or cryptocurrencies.
- The regulation of digital currency is optional. CBDC is one illustration of a digital coin that is under regulation. Digital currencies like Bitcoin and Ethereum are examples of unregulated ones. In contrast to cryptocurrencies, which are completely uncontrolled in all countries, most virtual currencies are ungoverned.
- Not all digital currencies have strong cryptography. Unlike virtual currencies, which may or may not utilize encryption to safeguard their networks, cryptocurrencies always use cryptography.

7.6. DO WE NEED NEW DIGITAL CURRENCIES? IF SO, WHO SHOULD ISSUE THEM?

First, let us discuss whether and from whom digital currencies are needed by the economy. It is understood that our economy is experiencing a technological revolution right now. It is now possible to collect, manage, and share enormous amounts of data thanks to new digital technology and increased online activity.

This has dramatically lowered the costs of many tasks. It has resulted in powerful, hyper-scalable applications that have disrupted entire industries – everything from taxis to print media. New players have entered the digital economy to provide these services.

Although improvements in communications and information technology have been ongoing for many years, truly significant developments have just recently come about. The COVID-19 epidemic might have hastened the speed of digital transformation even more.

The financial system and even the creation of money itself have been affected by the technological revolution. One such instance is that market-makers now have access to real-time prices at five-millisecond time intervals on the major FX platforms.

Project Rio, a new application for monitoring fast-paced markets developed at the BIS Innovation Hub, allows the entire market order book to be monitored every 100 milliseconds, or 36,000 times every hour.

The first point of entry into finance is the market for payment services, which are foundational to all economic activity.

Digital disruptors are drawn to payments because they require less capital than other financial services and the data they produce can be used to cross-sell products. It's not a surprise that there has been a surge in digital innovation in the payments sector, with new digital payment services being offered by established companies, huge internet companies, and fintech startups.

> Numerous advancements in the underpinning infrastructures of payments are built upon and have been under development for many years. For instance, harnessing technological progress, central banks around the world have instituted real-time gross settlement (RTGS) systems over the past decades. In the meantime, these systems' running hours have increased globally, and in certain places, they now run nearly nonstop.

Also on the retail side, innovation is rampant, and a growing number of economies – 51 by our last count – have fast retail payment systems, which allow 24/7 instant settlement of payments between households and businesses.

These include systems like the Unified Payment Interface (UPI) in India, CoDi in Mexico, PIX in Brazil and the Fed Now proposal in the US. Together, these improvements have demonstrated the adaptability of the current system, demonstrating successful public-private partnership innovations. However, nobody is required to follow the direction of the current monetary system. There have been numerous attempts to innovate in less conventional domains in addition to enhancements to established systems. Digital currencies are one such instance since they have the potential to replace both traditional account-based currency and actual cash.

As was already established, electronic deposits on a digital ledger have been the standard method of account-based money for decades. However, there have been requests for and initiatives to digitize all forms of currency, including cash. It is neither desirable nor realistic, in my opinion, to completely replace either bank accounts or cash. However, let's talk about what a further digitalization of money might entail.

Narayana Kocherlakota – one of the world's leading monetary theorists, former president of the Federal Reserve Bank of Minneapolis and a former Stanford professor – argued in a famous 1998 paper that "money is memory."

Money serves as a stand-in for a publicly visible and freely accessible mechanism that keeps track of who owes what to whom by replacing an otherwise complicated web of bilateral IOUs.

There are two options for the architecture of digital money based on the notion that money is the memory of the economy. Decisions regarding access and architecture must be made at these intersections. The memory must first be checked to make sure it is accurate everywhere and at all times. Assuming the integrity, security, and finality of the payment system is what this means in the context of payments.

The function of a central intermediary vs a decentralized governance structure affects how to do this. Second, guidelines must be established with the necessary privacy protections in place for determining who gets access to this information and under what circumstances. For the payment system to function properly, we must have both adequate identity and privacy.

If societies want digital money, the first fork in the road is the choice of operational architecture. Should the payment system rely on a trusted central authority (such as the central bank) to ensure integrity and finality? Or could it be based on a decentralized governance system, where the validity of a payment depends on achieving consensus among network participants on what counts as valid payments?

This is the concept behind Bitcoin. The system developed by Satoshi Nakamoto aims to achieve decentralized consensus without the use of a central middleman. However, it is evident in practice that Bitcoin functions more like a speculative asset than actual money. One contact recently told me that Bitcoin is "Tesla without the cars" – observers are fascinated by it, but the actual value backing is lacking. The Bitcoin network might be better understood as a group of online gamers who trade real money for virtual goods.

Although it claims to be a separate unit of account, prices cannot be fixed in bitcoin due to value swings. This lessens its value as a medium of trade and devalues it as a store of value. There is substantial evidence of price manipulation, and the structure of the Bitcoin market is unquestionably concentrated and opaque.

Investors must foremost be aware that Bitcoin may completely crash. Exchange cannot be guaranteed by scarcity or cryptography alone. Bitcoin requires the "proof of work" mechanism, which consumes a lot of energy, to securely process transactions.

The system's security is maintained by so-called miners, who are compensated with newly created currencies. The system consumes more electricity than the entire nation of Switzerland, which is a devastating side effect.

In the future, as Bitcoin approaches its maximum supply of 21 million coins, the "seigniorage" to miners will decline. And the system will be increasingly vulnerable to the "majority attacks" that are already plaguing smaller cryptocurrencies.

What then of so-called stable coins – cryptocurrencies that seek to stabilize their value against sovereign fiat currencies or another safe asset? Facebook's Libra – recently renamed Diem – was initially marketed as a "simple currency for billions."

Due to its peg to a group of reliable currencies like the US dollar and the euro, it would gain legitimacy. Diem has taken on new forms in recent years that resemble so-called e-money or other types of digital payment services and are pegged to certain sovereign currencies.

Compared to Bitcoin, this is undoubtedly more dependable. However, if a private organization produces its own currency and oversees maintaining the asset backing, there are still significant governance challenges. Historical examples demonstrate that there may be compelling reasons to stray from a sound asset underpinning, such as the need to invest in riskier assets in order to maximize profits.

In general, private stable coins cannot be the foundation of a stable monetary system. It is still possible that stable coins will have useful, specific use cases. But they must be strictly regulated and overseen if they are to maintain their credibility. They must build on the confidence and foundations already established by central banks to function inside the current financial system.

I side here with Milton Friedman, who argued, "Something like a moderately stable monetary framework seems an essential prerequisite for the effective operation of a private market economy. It is dubious that the market can by itself provide such a framework.

Hence, the function of providing one is an essential governmental function on a par with the provision of a stable legal framework." This idea remains as relevant as ever in the digital age.

Therefore, it is obvious that for digital money to exist, the central bank must play a crucial role in assuring the value's stability, the elasticity of the total supply of such money, and the system's overall security. Such a system cannot fail and cannot stand for any significant errors.

This refers once more to the idea that money serves as a record of societal economic connections and the yearning to belong. The same way that our memories are linked to the experiences we had relationships, so too does money not exist in a vacuum that is independent of economic interactions.

Long-term bonds are forged by economic interactions between borrowers and lenders, as well as between suppliers, intermediaries, and customers. Such a web of trading builds a reservoir of relationship-specific capital that supports financial connections, and it is this reservoir by which it is supported.

The traceability of the underlying transactions and the identification of all counterparties help to build up this capital. Historical examples demonstrate the importance of identification in fostering business.

For instance, in 18th-century Europe merchants used so-called bills of exchange to solve the lack of trust between physically remote lenders and borrowers. Instead of extending loans directly to borrowers in distant cities, merchants could plan with others whom they personally knew, creating a web connecting far-flung parties together.

Another example is the Maghreb traders of the 11th century. As Avner Greif – also of Stanford – famously showed, it was identity and traceability that allowed these traders to sustain trade, even over long distances and in the presence of great uncertainty.

The need of your virtual ID for receiving government benefits like pensions and cash transfers is even more evident today. The security of the payment system, fraud prevention, and support for AML/CFT (anti-money laundering (AML) and countering the financing of terrorism) all depend on some form of identification. Access and traceability can be compromised. Gaining greater knowledge has many positive social effects, such as reducing the likelihood of tax fraud or money laundering. Here, accurate identification can be helpful and provide law enforcement officials with new instruments to conduct their mandate.

Overall, I believe that a system that is entirely anonymous will not be effective. And most users would agree that their fundamental information would be retained with a reliable organization, like their bank or the government. Therefore, the concept of total anonymity is a myth.

Users leave a trace and share information today with financial intermediaries. This makes it easier for them to work online and prevent losses. To recount one recent anecdote, the user who lost his hard drive with $220 million of bitcoin would have liked to have a backup.

So, if we take the path, I have laid out just now, where do we end up? In my opinion, we will eventually have digital currencies issued by central banks that require some sort of identity, mostly through account-based access. Today, it is possible to create a central bank money representation that is technologically more advanced.

This can combine novel digital technologies with the tried-and-true characteristics of central banks – such as trust, transparency, legal backing, and finality – that others would need to either rely on or create for themselves from the ground up.

7.7. DESIGNING CBDCS FOR THE BENEFIT OF SOCIETIES

Digital currencies from central banks come in two different varieties. For payments between financial institutions and significant commercial participants, the first is in the wholesale sector. In the last few years, there has been a lot of activity around both private and central bank-issued wholesale digital currencies (Figure 7.3).

Efficiency improvements could result from these efforts, for example by enabling quicker settlement and delivery in comparison to payment. However, they might not be that disruptive. Once more, there is already digital central bank money for wholesale use in the form of central bank reserves.

Figure 7.3. CBDC.

Source: Image by Flickr.

It is important to note that privately issued wholesale digital currencies, also known as utility tokens or wholesale stable coins, are not actual independent currencies. They continue to rely on central banks to ensure that clearing and settlement are final. Like the stable currencies I previously stated, they remain "umbilical corded" to the current financial system.

The retail sector is where the true disruption of the second form of digital currency rests. Retail digital currencies might be used in everyday transactions by individuals, corporations, and governments, and depending on how they are built, they could completely transform our current financial system.

Central banks from all over the world were surveyed by the BIS regarding their interactions with CBDCs. Some focus exclusively on the wholesale side, while others focus largely on the retail side, but the majority are interested in both (center panel).

Increasingly, we see central banks moving beyond research towards actual pilots (right-hand panel). Since 2020, there has been a live CBDC, with the Sand Dollar project in the Bahamas. The People's Bank of China is performing large-scale pilots across China. And the Boston Fed is working with the MIT Digital Currency Initiative on retail CBDC research that will be open source, for all to review.

The reasons why central banks participate in CBDC activity vary between central banks and between retail and wholesale programs. But it is notable that safety and robustness are recognized as being a critical necessity in both scenarios, particularly for those central banks that have advanced beyond research towards proofs of concept or pilots.

Many central banks consider CBDC to guarantee that the public continues to have access to a secure, publicly issued payment option to supplement cash in the face of falling cash use and limited access to the banking system. Notably, central banks see opportunities in digital technologies, not least to enhance payments efficiency and promote financial inclusion. Thus, the question here is not so much "Do we need digital currencies?" but "Can central banks grasp the opportunity for what could be a technologically superior representation of central bank money?"

It is not intended that efforts in the private sector be replaced by work on CBDCs. Undoubtedly, we must benefit from innovation in the private sector, and the business sector is a vital partner in many research initiatives and pilot programs.

Disruptive innovation might pose a threat, but it can also present an opportunity, as the CBDC study demonstrates. Therefore, even with CBDC, central banks are remaining true to what money has always been: a social convention that involves a role for both the private sector and the central bank or other public bodies.

In this way, financial transactions are an example of a public-private cooperation. As a result, CBDCs can and must be created in a way that preserves the two-tiered financial system. We shouldn't just consider models where the central bank directly delivers retail services when considering private sector engagement (such as the Fed Accounts idea).

From a user perspective, a successful retail CBDC would need to provide a resilient and inclusive digital complement to physical cash – but that does not preclude an important role for the private sector.

The BIS is doing research into two-tier "Hybrid" and "Intermediated" CBDC designs that might make the private sector the default operator of payments with the central bank maintaining a backup infrastructure as an optional measure of added resilience.

Users could pay with a CBDC just as today, with a debit card, online banking tool or smartphone-based app, all operated by a bank or other private sector payment provider. However, instead of these intermediaries booking transactions on their own balance sheets as is the case today, they would simply update the record of who owns which CBDC balance.

An equivalent to cash claim on the central bank would be the CBDC itself. Through the continued provision of retail payment services by private sector intermediaries, the central bank is spared the operational duties of opening accounts and managing payments for consumers.

The advantage of using private sector intermediates is that there are no balance sheet issues. Additionally, these architectures enable the central bank to run backup systems if the private sector experiences technological difficulties. According to a BIS working paper that we are releasing today, a system that is like the current system in many aspects might operate effectively on distributed ledger technology (DLT). This chapter finds that despite all the limitations with Bitcoin and other permission less cryptocurrencies, greater economic promise lies with the "permissioned" variant of DLT.

In permissioned DLT, a known network of validators replaces the traditional model with one central validator. In a proof of concept that entailed settling tokenized assets with central bank money using DLT-based software, the BIS Innovation Hub has already shown that this is possible in a lab setting.

The working paper demonstrates that the technology may have commercial viability outside of the lab, primarily in niche industries. It demonstrates that while a trusted central intermediary outperforms both permissioned and permission-less DLT, the latter offers more promise.

Thus, DLT can only outperform the conventional model of centralized exchange in situations where there is a lack of confidence in the rule of law and its ability to be upheld. In addition to the system's administration, it's important to pay attention to the rules governing how users can access the system.

What about the role of identification, and of the transaction data that digital currencies will generate? Here, we need to compare different governance rules and analyze the role of the public and the private sector in guarding data.

Naturally, taking precautions is necessary given the risk of data breaches or misuse by governmental bodies. However, there are designs where some degree of individual privacy may be maintained – a CBDC does not have to mean an Orwellian Big Brother, where the central bank views every transaction.

As settlement agents in a competitive payment system, private sector intermediaries have a part to play in this as well. Private intermediaries could (temporarily) record and protect user data. However, choices regarding data privacy are crucial.

This is not merely a technological problem; it is also a significant policy one that goes beyond the realm of finance. In this regard, central banks must pay attention to the needs of society. Additionally, there will still be a need for oversight from the public sector and transparent mechanisms for data governance. It must be made sure that one institution is ultimately accountable to the user if numerous parties are engaged in the data collection, transfer, and storage processes. If this is done well, a system like todays might assist protect privacy while granting law enforcement access in accordance with well-defined guidelines.

Moreover, it could put competitive pressure on today's intermediaries, pushing for more efficiency, lower costs, and better service in payment markets.

7.8. WHAT IS BITCOIN?

At first sight, the question in the headline might appear stupid, yet it has a (apparently) simple solution. When discussing bitcoin, users, and advocates typically refer to it as cryptocurrency, which is currency that is encrypted. Other times, they refer to it as a virtual currency or, more specifically, as money (Figure 7.4).

Figure 7.4. Bitcoin.

Source: Image by Peakpx.

The first definition, which can be found on portal dedicated to Bitcoin, states "Bitcoin is an innovative payment network and a new kind of money."

7.8.1. Bitcoin and Theoretical Definition of Money

Answering the question in the form of a clear statement "bitcoin is money" is not entirely unproblematic. The theoretical definition of money considers money as "any asset that is generally accepted for payment for goods or services, or for debt settlement" (Revenda et al., 2005).

The concept and the demand for universal acceptability are incongruent in the case of Bitcoin. We cannot speak of widespread adoption, even though the rate of Bitcoin usage is rising with time. The Bitcoin community of users who accept Bitcoin as money must be defined if we are to make an argument in its favor.

We all agree that currencies like the Indonesian Rupiah are forms of money, yet it is obvious that making purchases in the Czech Republic would be quite challenging (and equally difficult it would be to convert IDR in CZK).

Such argument, however, is misunderstood due to omission of definition distinction between "money" and "currency." National currency is a form of money (Revenda et al., 2005) and therefore we can talk about the general acceptance of the Indonesian Rupiah in Indonesia, the Czech koruna in Czech Republic, but the same cannot be said about Bitcoin, which is not legal tender in any country.

It is unable to escape this definitional trap by providing a precise definition of the users' community. The group is quite welcoming, and anyone who wants to join can do so. Accepting Bitcoin is the sole shared trait.

If we adopted this definition of generosity, practically everything that is currently accepted by a small number of people as a value of exchange could become money. The notion of money as an asset is the second area where Bitcoin runs into trouble with the theoretical definition of money.

If the money for the user is an asset, it is logically implied that the issuer constitutes a liability, obligation, which must be satisfied. Although there is a legal relationship today, the central bank cannot be required to demand the exchange of issued money for another asset. Nonetheless, this relationship is shown in the central bank's balance sheet.

That doesn't apply to Bitcoin in any way. The recipient places received Bitcoin to the side of its assets as payment for the service obtained in the form of system operation, and since the central authority is missing, a comparable accounting record in the issuer balance sheet is also missing. New bitcoins are issued on established algorithms, from formal (accounting) point of view "from nothing."

7.8.2. Bitcoin and Empirical Definition of Money

Modern monetary theories also use empirical definitions of money because the theoretical definition is restricted to legal tender only. The empirical definition of money seeks to address the connection between the quantitative growth of money and other macroeconomic factors.

As such, in addition to providing a definition of money, it also addresses the issues of what constitutes money and what is not considered to be money. The amount of money with a specific level of liquidity is represented by monetary aggregates, which are built to track the evolution (Revenda et al., 2005).

The empirical definition faces significant challenges in the case of Bitcoin. What bitcoin is and is not is very apparent. Bitcoin does not have a strong connection to the banking system, hence no securities or term deposits issued in Bitcoin exist.

Since Bitcoin is always usable, making distinctions based on the degree of liquidity is pointless. Regarding liquidity, bitcoin can be compared to cash in bank current accounts; more specifically, when it comes to the rapidity of transfers, we can refer to bitcoin as "virtual currency."

Therefore, it is apparent that Bitcoin belongs in M1, but no additional bitcoin-related monetary aggregates exist. It is quite difficult to know how many bitcoins are or are not in use. Both the total amount of bitcoins that will be issued and the number of bitcoins that are now being issued are known.

This does not mean that all existing bitcoins are in circulation. It is not even a matter of possible bitcoin savings, i.e., the amount of money that is not deliberately used (like a standard cash money at home in the mattress). The amount of bitcoin is reduced by losses.

There could be a destruction of the entire data repository to relevant bitcoin account, or the access is lost. Publicly known is the case of a British man, James Howells, who threw his computer disk wallet containing 7,500 Bitcoin out and then searched for it at the local landfill (Novinky.cz, 2013).

Your ability to access the appropriate wallet will also be lost if you forget your password. This effectively takes any held bitcoins out of circulation. While the central bank can renew cash money and anybody can request access to a current account (allowing the bank to use the money stored there for economic purposes), these restrictions do not apply to Bitcoin.

Although the amount of bitcoin that can be used in the economy is unknown, it is possible to predict that there will be fewer of them available once bitcoin emissions stop.

7.8.3. Bitcoin and Law Definition of Money

The legal term is the last definition I'd like to offer regarding money. Each nation has its own definition of legal tender, and both developed (the United States, the European Union, including the Czech Republic) and developing (other countries) economies have debates concerning the legitimacy of virtual currencies like Bitcoin (China).

Czech law serves as an illustration of how bitcoin, which its users surely assume to be money, does not adhere to the requirements for the legal category of money. The Czech Payment Services Act defines electronic money by following criteria: Electronic money is monetary value that:

- represents a claim to the issuer;
- is stored on an electronic means of payment;
- is issued against receiving of funds in the value not less than the value of issued electronic money;
- is accepted as means of payment by persons other than the issuer.

Bitcoin does not meet criteria to be included in the category of electronic money. As mentioned above, bitcoin does not represent for issuer a liability in its balance sheet and therefore we cannot talk about bitcoins as a claim of the owner to the issuer.

The requirement to issue electronic currency only after receiving funds draws attention to this issue. There is never such a transaction. The nature of the publication precludes considering bitcoin as electronic money.

Only banks, foreign banks, or their branches, domestic or foreign credit unions or foreign electronic money institutions, electronic money issuers of small extent or Czech Central Bank can issue electronic money (from legal point of view).

Based on the issuance of an electronic money agreement, the institutions for electronic money are permitted to issue electronic money (Schlossberger, 2012). A decentralized system like Bitcoin that lacks institutional operators cannot meet this requirement.

What is Bitcoin according to the Czech law? Since Bitcoin does not fit the requirements of any category of money, its inclusion in other categories is necessary. The second category that naturally springs to mind is security, however while Bitcoin is traded similarly on stock exchanges, it is not according to Czech law a security.

Bitcoin does not have any rights attached to it that may be represented. There is also the issue of whether bitcoin is a commodity. In contrast to other commodities, it is impossible to associate Bitcoin with any form of consumption. The use for other exchange is the sole option.

Bitcoin cannot be referred as a commodity at all. The Czech law no. 89/2012 Coll. § 489 defines a thing as everything what is different from the person and serves to satisfy the needs of people. Because of bitcoin having no physical substance, it can be considered as an intangible thing as Czech law stated which is storable on a tangible medium in electronic form.

According to Czech law, the inclusion under fee stamps of peculiar kind is another potential description of Bitcoin (fee stamps sui generis). Fee stamps are defined as a form of payment that replaces money acquired via the payment of an amount equivalent to their nominal value.

Another issue is figuring out what the nominal value of Bitcoin is. Unlike a tax stamp, for instance, bitcoin does not have a nominal value specified in Czech crowns.

From the point of view of common sense, we could consider the transaction of bitcoin purchase as money exchange (buying one bitcoin for another bitcoin does not make sense, the direct value against any other currency is not determined, the price is a result of market supply and demand). Therefore, bitcoin must be referred as fee stamp of special kind (Vrbíková, 2014, p. 138).

Bitcoin is prohibited by statutory provisions and official declarations made by pertinent organizations. The Czech Central Bank specifically stated in a statement on bitcoin that trading with bitcoin does not require a central bank permit and is not regulated by the central bank.

That would only occur if there were a movement of cashless money or electronic money between buyers and sellers during the arrangement of trades using bitcoins, while managing funds invested in bitcoins, or when executing payment operations in conjunction with those trades (this definition does not include transfer of money against bitcoins).

The declaration does, however, contain a warning that explicitly states that routinely refusing to accept domestic currency in exchange for goods and services is illegal. But there is no issue with accepting Bitcoin in exchange for goods and services. The Ministry of Finance's Financial-Analytical department's methodological guidance about how liable parties should interact with digital currencies uses the risk of digital currency as a means of potentially disrupting the flow of cash. Since there is no definition provided, the use of bitcoin as a payment mechanism is more widely understood.

According to the guideline, any payment in excess of 1,000 EUR is perceived as "very risky" and as a suspicious transaction and each transaction with a value higher than EUR 15,000 must be reported (Financial-Analytical Department, 2013).

A misunderstanding of German legal peculiarities led to the recognition of Bitcoin as money in German law. As legal cash or a foreign currency, bitcoin is not accepted in Germany. Only the "accounting unit" requirement is met by bitcoin. In German law, "accounting unit" is equivalent to "FX," but with the distinction that it is not recognized as a legitimate form of payment.

This category includes items that are used in private contracts as private means of payment for a certain user group. As a result, "private money" can be used to describe bitcoins. This categorization is a compromise and most accurately captures the nature of Bitcoin use.

At the same time, however, this inclusion implies the need to pay sales tax when trading with Bitcoin (Deutscher Bundestag, 2013). Due to the reflection of European law into Czech law it is not surprising that bitcoin does not meet the definition criteria of electronic money according to European directive on electronic money (2009/110/EC) from the same reasons as in Czech law.

The Payment Services Directive (2007/64/EC), which may also be significant for classifying bitcoin. This directive depends on how the electronic money directive is defined, and as a result, bitcoin once more falls outside of this definition's bounds. Even on a European scale, bitcoin does not fall under the umbrella of money and is technically not classified as having a distinct status (ECB, 2012).

According to the definition given by the ECB in their research, virtual currency is "a sort of uncontrolled digital money, which is subscribed to and typically controlled by their developers and utilized and acknowledged by the unique virtual community." (ECB, 2012).

This, however, is merely a conceptual explanation and not the formal definition according to the law. According to the ECB definition, bitcoin is a type of virtual currency scheme with a two-way flow. This represents the reality that bitcoin may be converted into and out of legal money and used to buy goods and services in the actual economy (ECB, 2012).

7.9. BITCOIN AND STORE OF VALUE MONEY FUNCTION

Money has widely recognized and acknowledged purposes. There is only one difference between the various financial functions. Jevons in his book from 1875 "Money and the Mechanism of Exchange" defines four basic functions of money: Medium of exchange, common measure of value, standard of value and store of value. In the current theory of money occur other money functions like information function, investment function, etc. (Jedlinský, 2014).

Jevons uses the following justification to show how important it is to understand the role that money plays as a store of value: "But sometimes a person needs to condense his property into the smallest compass, so that he may hoard it away for a while, carry it with him on a long journey, or transmit it to a friend in a far-off country" (Jevons, 2011).

Of course, there are better ways to send goods to a friend in another nation, and using Bitcoin is one of them. However, the necessity to store property is a crucial component of the economy. People must learn to live with the knowledge that their salaries are fluctuating over time and save money now for potential future hardships (Figure 7.5).

Figure 7.5. Most popular cryptocurrencies.

Source: Image by Space Coast Daily.

The act of purchasing items that are more expensive than one's normal pay indicates the function of value storage. Graham (1940), who identifies just two primary purposes of money: money as an accounting unit and money as a bearer of options, makes a counterargument against store of value. These fundamental functions are the sources of all other functions.

Graham stated that "Many other things, easy to store, easy to move, and of reasonable vendibility, provide a more than acceptable substitute for money in this respect" (Graham, 1940, p. 2). The need to hold money still exists, thus Graham did not completely abolish the store of value function; it is simply explained as temporary holding and is incorporated in the bearer of option function.

Fiat currencies are criticized by bitcoin proponents for having an inflationary nature. The central banks that control the currency that my governments use run the risk of "creating money," which would cause it to depreciate. Supporters of Bitcoin believe that fiat currencies do not fulfill the purpose of a store of value, and that virtual currencies are the most competitive in this regard.

There is also the argument that whole success of virtual currencies is based on the fact of non-inflation character.

7.10. ON THE VALUE OF VIRTUAL CURRENCIES

Virtual currencies, like Bitcoin, signify the advent of a brand-new type of money as well as a brand-new method of making payments for products and services. These currencies might be outside the reach of the present financial institutions.

In other words, their availability is not always regulated by central banks, and they enable consumers and businesses to transact with one another directly and without the use of any financial intermediaries over distance. The crucial development is the incorporation of cryptographic identification methods into a "distributed ledger," or a digital record that enables the tracking and certification of all payments made.

This allows virtual currencies to be used in a decentralized payment system while avoiding the possibility of "double spending."

According to our estimate, the introduction of a potentially successful virtual currency will result in a sharp spike in the exchange rate driven by speculative intentions. Furthermore, according to our model, high levels of volatility resemble "growing pains" because during the early adoption stage, when few real payments are settled in virtual currency and speculation is one of the main reasons to own virtual currency, the exchange rate is particularly sensitive to shifts in speculators' beliefs.

Theoretically, as more customers and businesses use payments, volatility is predicted to decline. Time will tell how much volatility will decrease. Virtual currency's constant supply may mean that, as compared to traditional currencies, whose quantities are controlled by central banks, its volatility will be more akin to that of other commodities (e.g., Selgin 2014).

Additionally, while Bitcoin's most popular virtual currency's exchange rate volatility typically declining, it is still three times higher than the volatility of the price of gold.

Bitcoin is the most well-known virtual currency for primers on the economics behind Bitcoin; see, for example, Dwyer (2015); and Bohme et al. (2015). Bitcoin ¨ was launched in 2009 and attracted attention from the financial press, economists, central banks, and governments.

This attention was fueled by the sudden "explosion" and volatility in the exchange rate of Bitcoin by the end of 2013. In November 2013, the U.S.-dollar exchange rate for one unit of Bitcoin increased more than fivefold. Bitcoins had begun trading for less than a nickel in 2010; by November 2013, the exchange rate exceeded $1,100.

During 2014, however, the exchange rate quickly lost ground again, settling at around $250 in March 2015, after which its value rose to $4,300 per bitcoin in September 2017. While the supply of Bitcoin units over time is mathematically specified with an upper limit of 21 million units, its current supply amounts to approximately 16.6 million units (in September 2017).

The usage of bitcoin is still relatively low, but it is growing from 20,000 daily transactions in 2012 to over 70,000 daily transactions in 2014, and then to an average of approximately 2,50,000 daily transactions in September 2017. Overall, Bitcoin is currently a very modest monetary phenomenon compared to the volume and value of other currencies, although it has been expanding.

To study the early adoption stage exchange rate of virtual currency and its primary drivers, this research proposes an economic framework. Our model will take into account several crucial characteristics of the most popular virtual currencies—Bitcoin in particular.

First, since merchants typically quickly update price quotes in virtual currency to the most recent available exchange rate, virtual currency prices of goods and services are completely flexible with respect to changes in the conversion rate.

This characteristic of the model is essential for establishing a clear connection between the demand for virtual money and the exchange rate. Secondly, choosing to use virtual currency for payments also means choosing an alternate transaction technology, as these payments are settled and processed through a peer-to-peer payment network linked to that virtual currency.

The final demand for virtual currency is heavily influenced by network economies that influence payment options. Third, many virtual currencies have predetermined growth rules that cause their supply to rise. A major source of uncertainty in our model will be the future demand for virtual money to perform payments, in keeping with this latter characteristic.

Our analysis shows how the exchange rate of virtual currency is determined when prices in virtual currency are perfectly flexible with respect to changes in the exchange rate while prices in fiat money are determined in the rest of the world. Perfect flexibility of prices with respect to the exchange rate is not a unique property of virtual currency in the early-adoption stage.

It may also characterize a traditional currency facing extremely high and volatile inflation, when price setting occurs in practice in terms of a stable (foreign) currency (such as the U.S. dollar); see, for example, Dornbusch, Sturzenegger, & Wolf (1990).

However, a key distinction is that investors have no incentives to hold a highly inflating currency as a store of wealth, whereas speculation is commonly accepted as one of the motivations for holding virtual currency.

Therefore, from a financial standpoint, virtual currency in its early stages of adoption offers an intriguing case study for monitoring speculative demand for a currency and complete flexibility of prices in relation to the exchange rate.

Our framework combines an investor's portfolio model with a payment network model, while adding a flavor of monetary economics. In our framework, three components are important for the exchange rate:

- the current usage of virtual currency to make real payments;
- the decision and expectations of forward-looking investors to buy virtual currency (thereby effectively regulating its supply); and
- the elements that jointly drive future consumer adoption and merchant acceptance of virtual currency.

These latter factors affect the anticipated long-term increase in virtual currency usage. We demonstrate that the equilibrium exchange rate depends on both a "purely speculative" component, which is based on the hypothetical price that traders would offer if not a single real transaction were settled using virtual currency, and a transaction component, which is based on the actual amount required to enable real payments.

Speculating on the value of currencies is not new. In the early 1900s, Fisher (1911) argued that, in certain situations, speculators may effectively regulate the money supply by withdrawing money from circulation when betting on its future value.

We put this "ancient" idea into practice in a formal fashion by demonstrating how the value of a virtual currency varies in response to changes in investors' speculative positions. Our model predicts that as a virtual currency gains acceptance, the exchange rate will become less sensitive to the effects of shocks to speculators' perceptions and their influx and outflow from the market for virtual currencies.

This forecast casts doubt on the claim that the widespread use of virtual currencies will be prevented in the long run by the excessive volatility of their exchange values at present.

7.11. VIRTUAL CURRENCY CONCERNS AND REGULATORY IMPLICATIONS

7.11.1. Price Volatility

One main deterrent to the proliferation of virtual currencies is price volatility. The decentralized nature of many virtual currencies means they lack a stability mechanism to curb price fluctuations; theoretically, you could go from holding $100 to $50 worth of Bitcoins overnight.

Therefore, it might not be a good idea to retain virtual currencies for an extended period of time, such as for portfolio diversification.

However, consumers can acquire and spend virtual currency within minutes when utilizing them as an instant form of payment, including when making remittances, which significantly lowers the risk of price fluctuation.

The creation of a supportive environment for virtual currency businesses to thrive could be the goal of future governments. Standards on periods of exposure to currency risk could be implemented in order to make virtual money a more sustainable and useful form of both payment and investment in the long run. Governments can encourage innovation and competition in the technologies that provide financial services and alternative payment methods by funding the study, creation, and use of new virtual currency technologies.

Eventually, the value of virtual currency tokens should stabilize as more people begin to use them, since the greater the user base, the less effect each person has on impacting the price.

7.11.2. Potential for Illegal Activity

The security protocols used by virtual currency networks have developed and grown along with those communities. Many threats still exist, though. The most urgent risks include the susceptibility of systems using virtual currencies to hacking and other security lapses, as well as the anonymity they grant users, which can be used for bad intentions.

Online illegal markets like Silk Road may flourish if the Deep Web is not properly regulated. Like the rest of the globe, Asia, and the Pacific have a variety of legislative frameworks for virtual currencies, ranging from endorsement to basic acceptance to outright rejection.

The Government of China, concerned about the use of Bitcoin in capital flight and tax evasion, has restricted Bitcoin exchanges. Private people can hold Bitcoins, but financial companies cannot. Regulators are introducing regulations on cryptocurrency companies in the Republic of Korea.

Initial coin offerings (ICOs), a kind of fund-raising in which investors are given cryptocurrency tokens, are prohibited in China and the Republic of Korea because they are viewed as being extremely speculative.

Japan, on the other hand, has officially recognized Bitcoin as a legal method of payment, in an apparent bid to become the global center of FinTech. There are no regulations with respect to its transaction or possession in Thailand, India, Indonesia, Viet Nam, Philippines, or Singapore.

Regulation is becoming necessary as virtual currencies spread throughout society. The capability of their law enforcement agencies to recognize and effectively address the illegitimate use of virtual money both inside and beyond borders should be evaluated and improved, according to policymakers.

Government authorities should be given the resources, training, and legal framework they need to identify and deal with illicit usage of virtual currencies, according to policymakers. Depending on how virtual currencies are categorized, different regulatory, legal, and tax systems will apply (i.e., as a currency or as an asset).

Government officials might also enact laws against money laundering that would apply to virtual currency exchanges in their nations and collaborate with the sector to develop voluntary consumer protection guidelines.

Finally, to address the regulatory challenges surrounding virtual currency use, governments could collaborate with global entities such as the financial action task force (FATF), as well as with other countries.

7.12. INTERRELATION BETWEEN VIRTUAL CURRENCIES AND DISTRIBUTED COORDINATION

The history of a brand-new monetary phenomena, subsequently referred to as "virtual currency," is closely related to the creation of Bitcoin as the first publicly coordinated validation network. This is understandable, given that the network's creator, who dubbed it a "Peer-to-Peer Electronic Cash System," invented the story.

However, the distribution of a virtual currency as a common characteristic is not only shared by self-declared distributed payment systems. Rather, this technical feature is functionally interrelated to publicly coordinated infrastructure in the form of an incentive mechanism.

The network participants must make sure that their ledger is accurate and consistent in the absence of a reliable intermediary. The participants' ability to manipulate the ledger in their own benefit, such as if they were able to spend their virtual money twice (the so-called "double-spending dilemma"), would compromise the integrity of their coordination system.

Even if most participants of the respective coordination system are trustworthy, an attacker could establish a large amount of fake network nodes to undermine the voting procedure (so called "Sybil attack"). The consensus mechanism introduced by Satoshi Nakamoto was the first scalable solution to that coordination challenge.

However, the verification process, also known as "proof of work," in the context of Bitcoin and the majority of other distributed ledgers, necessitates that participant's work through a so-called hash function, which entails solving cryptographic problems.

Accordingly, transactions can only be performed based on a sizeable quantity of computer power that the participants must contribute to the relevant network. This achieves the goal of reducing the possible advantages of fraudulent activity to those that are less than the costs that increase with the network's overall computational capability.

However, the result of this arrangement is that it needs an incentive structure that motivates the members to contribute their computational resources to the network for it to attain a sufficient level of integrity and be used as a reliable coordination system.

In fact, an effective joint management of common infrastructure (such as the public coordination platform described here) cannot rely on an altruistic motivation of the community but must be based on game-theoretic approach.

This is where the creation of virtual currencies comes into play, even if given the significant exchange rate fluctuation, their ability to act as a store of value may be constrained. The distribution of virtual currency acts as a form of payment for participation in the coordinating process, enabling the participants to pay for the upkeep of the expensive hardware and to make money.

In addition, without a central bank, the reward function sets the conditions under which units of account enter the monetary system. Werbach noted that even in the instance of Bitcoin, the functional interplay between distributed coordination and the production of virtual money is ambiguous: "Bitcoins are thus both the output and input of the system."

One could equally well describe Bitcoin as a trust infrastructure designed to support a digital currency, or a digital currency designed to support a trust infrastructure.

Put differently, the respective user is the one who adjusts the focus either on the payment function or on another application on the grounds of the more general coordination function of the network.

7.13. CONCLUSION

This chapter provided a summary of information on virtual money used in virtual worlds. The chapter began with an introduction, then went on to describe the various forms of virtual currencies and their benefits and drawbacks.

In the middle of the chapter, we covered the difference between digital currencies, virtual currencies, and crypto currencies and covered questions like – do we need new digital currencies? If so, who should issue them? And what is Bitcoin?

The chapter's final section covered the function of bitcoin as a store of value, the worth of virtual currencies, potential regulatory issues, and the relationship between virtual currencies and distributed coordination.

REFERENCES

1. Bolt, W., & Oordt, M. V., (2019). *(PDF) On the Value of Virtual Currencies*. researchgate.net. Available at: https://www.researchgate.net/publication/332557875_On_the_Value_of_Virtual_Currencies (accessed on 15 June 2023).
2. Carstens, A., (2021). *Digital Currencies and the Future of the Monetary System*. The Bank for International Settlements. Available at: https://www.bis.org/speeches/sp210127.htm (accessed on 15 June 2023).
3. Frankenfield, J., (2022). *Virtual Currency: Definition, Types, Advantages & Disadvantages*. Investopedia. Available at: https://www.investopedia.com/terms/v/virtual-currency.asp#:~:text=Virtual%20currencies%20are%20digital%20representations%20of%20value%20that%20can%20exist,as%20such%2C%20are%20mostly%20unregulated (accessed on 15 June 2023).
4. Hofert, E., (2019). *Regulating Virtual Currencies*. econstor.eu. Institute for Monetary and Financial Stability. Available at: https://www.econstor.eu/bitstream/10419/191053/1/1046474618.pdf (accessed on 15 June 2023).
5. Kubát, M., (2015). *Virtual Currency Bitcoin in the Scope of Money Definition and Store of Value*. core.ac.uk. Elsevier. Available at: https://core.ac.uk/download/pdf/82400847.pdf (accessed on 15 June 2023).
6. *The Economic and Social Commission for Asia and the Pacific,* (n.d.). unescap.org. ESCAP. Available at: https://www.unescap.org/sites/default/files/ESCAP_DV_Currency_0.pdf (accessed on 15 June 2023).
7. *Virtual Currency,* (2022). Corporate Finance Institute. Available at: https://corporatefinanceinstitute.com/resources/cryptocurrency/virtual-currency/ (accessed on 15 June 2023).
8. *What are Virtual Currencies?* (n.d.). www.cftc.gov. CFTC. Available at: https://www.cftc.gov/sites/default/files/2019-12/oceo_aivc0218.pdf (accessed on 15 June 2023).

INDEX

C